DISCARD

MADONNA

MADONNA

A Biography

Mary Cross

GREENWOOD BIOGRAPHIES

GREENWOOD PRESS
WESTPORT, CONNECTICUT • LONDON

Library of Congress Cataloging-in-Publication Data

Cross, Mary, 1934–
    Madonna : a biography / Mary Cross.
      p. cm. — (Greenwood biographies, ISSN 1540-4900)
    Includes bibliographical references and index.
    ISBN–13: 978–0–313–33811–3 (alk. paper)
    ISBN–10: 0–313–33811–6 (alk. paper)
    1. Madonna, 1958– 2. Singers—United States—Biography. I. Title.
    ML420.M1387C76 2007
    782.42166092–dc22
    [B]   2007000542

British Library Cataloguing in Publication Data is available.

Library of Congress Catalog Card Number: 2007000542

ISBN–13: 978–0–313–33811–3
ISBN–10: 0–313–33811–6
ISSN: 1540–4900

First published in 2007

Greenwood Press, 88 Post Road West, Westport, CT 06881
An imprint of Greenwood Publishing Group, Inc.
www.greenwood.com

Printed in China

∞™

The paper used in this book complies with the
Permanent Paper Standard issued by the National
Information Standards Organization (Z39.48–1984).

10 9 8 7 6 5 4 3 2 1

To my four daughters

CONTENTS

Photo essay begins after page 66.

SERIES FOREWORD

In response to high school and public library needs, Greenwood developed this distinguished series of full-length biographies specifically for student use. Prepared by field experts and professionals, these engaging biographies are tailored for high school students who need challenging yet accessible biographies. Ideal for secondary school assignments, the length, format, and subject areas are designed to meet educators' requirements and students' interests.

Greenwood offers an extensive selection of biographies spanning all curriculum related subject areas including social studies, the sciences, literature and the arts, history and politics, as well as popular culture, covering public figures and famous personalities from all time periods and backgrounds, both historical and contemporary, who have made an impact on American and/or world culture. Greenwood biographies were chosen based on comprehensive feedback from librarians and educators. Consideration was given to both curriculum relevance and inherent interest. The result is an intriguing mix of the well known and the unexpected, the saints and sinners from long-ago history and contemporary pop culture. Readers will find a wide array of subject choices from fascinating crime figures like Al Capone to inspiring pioneers like Margaret Mead, from the greatest minds of our time like Stephen Hawking to the most amazing success stories of our day like J. K. Rowling.

Although the emphasis is on fact, not glorification, the books are meant to be fun to read. Each volume provides in-depth information about the subject's life from birth through childhood, the teen years, and adulthood. A thorough account relates family background and education, traces personal and professional influences, and explores struggles, accomplishments, and contributions. A timeline highlights the most significant life events against a historical perspective. Bibliographies supplement the reference value of each volume.

INTRODUCTION

Who's that girl?

Who is Madonna, really?

Madonna has always defied attempts to pin down her identity by rapidly changing her image. She acts out our fantasies faster than we can dream them; her many personae taking center stage while she herself eludes capture.

We can scrutinize the biographical facts—birth, marriage, motherhood, career—and yet the real person, one of the world's most famous women, eludes us.

"You will never know the real me. Ever," she told *Vanity Fair* magazine at the height of her fame.[1]

The masks and the fantasy identities are profitable, certainly, keeping her fans wanting more. And they have inspired university professors and cultural critics to enshrine her as a postmodern icon of pastiche and appropriation. But lately Madonna has been trying out some new identities, seemingly for real. Take her new identity as wife to a member of the British gentry and as the mother of three children, living in the English countryside as if to the manor born. She has learned to ride horses and shoot quail, to run a large household with servants, and to embrace a domestic role as a wife and mother bringing up her son and daughter, as well as their new brother from Malawi.[2]

This is a long way from the MTV video Madonna of "Express Yourself" and "Justify My Love"; yet, new and different as it is, this may be a more authentic transformation for her. It is not about selling song-and-dance or even an image, although this new image doesn't hurt and it's not a transformation taking place in private. To drum up interest in her worldwide

Confessions on a Dance Floor tour in 2006 and those to come, Madonna has even been talking to the media about her new life, riding horseback with David Letterman, making pronouncements about child care, and appearing in the gossip columns and on the covers of fashion magazines on a regular basis. The video of her Number 1 song in 2006, "Hung Up," has received five MTV nominations, and she's given us another look at her backstage and private life in a new documentary, *I've Got a Secret to Tell You.* At the age of 48, keeping herself in the public eye and on the charts is more important than ever.

Madonna still projects her trademark saint and sinner image and still uses outrage to get attention. Of course, now that her children are old enough to ask questions about things like that outfit Mommy is wearing in that *Sex* book, it will be interesting to see how she handles melding her older image with her new one as a mother. Madonna says she is being very strict with her children, much as her father was with her. This means no ice cream or television, and punishment for tantrums over clothes.[3] She has written six children's books, offered one Christmas in a special boxed set by the luxury New York City store, Bergdorf Goodman, complete with a CD of Madonna reading the stories. Daughter Lourdes—the child Madonna had with trainer Carlos Leon in 1996—is 10 years old now and goes to a private school in London. Madonna's son Rocco—the child she had in 2000 with her now second husband, Guy Ritchie—is 6. Madonna seems, at the moment, to be reveling in her role as wife and mother, and perhaps it is a very authentic moment in the evolution of her persona.

Her new documentary, *I've Got a Secret to Tell You,* is as elusive as ever about who Madonna really is. No secrets are really revealed and the album titled *Confessions* does not deliver any actual confessions. Perhaps the identity of this fascinating woman, as she predicted, will never be plumbed to our satisfaction. The biographer's task, to unearth the life and the personality, seems daunting in the face of the many masks of Madonna. Yet we can speculate and do some detective work by looking at the "back story," starting with Madonna's life growing up in a big family in the Midwest.

NOTES

1. Quoted by Lynn Hirschberg, "The Misfit," *Vanity Fair,* April 1991. 168.

2. Hamish Bowles, "Like a Duchess," *Vogue,* August 2005. 230–240; 274.

3. Campbell Robertson, "Madonna and Friends: A Guide for Perplexed Parents," *The New York Times,* October 23, 2005. sec.4:4.

TIMELINE OF EVENTS IN THE LIFE OF MADONNA

August 16, 1958	Madonna Louise Ciccone is born in Bay City, Michigan. Lives in Pontiac, Michigan until she is 10.
1963	Begins grade school at St. Frederick's School in Pontiac, Michigan.
December 1, 1966	Mother dies of breast cancer. Father remarries; Joan Gustafson becomes Madonna's stepmother.
1967	Madonna is confirmed into the Catholic church at age 9; takes confirmation name of Veronica.
1968	Family moves to Rochester Hills, Michigan; Madonna transfers to St. Andrew's School in Rochester Hills, Michigan.
1969	Joan Gustafson Ciccone formally adopts Ciccone children.
1970	Begins junior high at West Junior High School in Rochester Hills, Michigan.
1972	Begins high school at Rochester Adams High School in Rochester Hills, Michigan; takes dance lessons at the Rochester School of Ballet.
1976	Wins dance scholarship to the University of Michigan in Ann Arbor, Michigan; enrolls that fall.
1978	Drops out of the university and moves to New York City in July to pursue dance career.

1978   Works at Dunkin Donuts, is associated with
              Pearl Lang's Dance Company and the Alvin
              Alley workshop briefly.

1979   Scrounges meals and lodgings in downtown
              Manhattan.

May 1979   Signs as backup dancer with disco star Patrick
              Hernandez; goes to Paris.

July 1979   Abandons Paris, returns to New York City, moves
              in with boyfriend Dan Gilroy and his brother in
              Queens; learns to play drums and guitar.

1980   Forms a band, The Breakfast Club, with Gilroy
              brothers, playing drums. Band performs at
              Country Bluegrass Blues Band (CBGB), other
              downtown clubs.
              Plays the lead in New York University student
              film, A Certain Sacrifice. Film was released in
              1985 against Madonna's wishes.

November 1980 Steve Bray, Madonna's Ann Arbor boyfriend,
              joins the band at her request. Bray plays drums
              and helps Madonna write songs and make a
              demo tape. Madonna moves to singing, rather
              than dancing.

1981   Partners with Mark Kamins, Danceteria disc
              jockey, who brokers a record deal for Madonna
              with Sire Records, a division of Warner
              Brothers.

March 1981   Madonna's band, now called Emmy, plays Max's
              Kansas City club twice with Madonna as lead
              singer.
              Madonna signs contract to make recordings
              with Gotham Records. Camille Barbone is her
              manager.

1982   Madonna meets John "Jellybean" Benitez, disc
              jockey at the Funhouse; they begin a three-year
              relationship.

February 1982 Madonna breaks contract and leaves Barbone
              and Gotham Records.

October 1982 Madonna's first single, "Everybody," released by
              Sire Records, makes the Billboard Hot 100 list.

1983   "Burning Up" and "Holiday" singles released
              from Madonna album.

July 1983	Debut album, *Madonna*, released by Sire/Warner Brothers, becomes a Top 5 hit, certified platinum by August 1984.
1984	Signs Freddy DeMann to be her manager. *Borderline*, MTV video, directed by Mary Lambert. "Lucky Star," written by Madonna, becomes Top 5 hit. *Lucky Star*, MTV video, directed by Arthur Pierson *Like a Virgin* video, directed by Mary Lambert, filmed in Venice.
January 1984	Appears on Dick Clark's "American Bandstand"; sings "Holiday."
September 1984	Madonna sings "Like a Virgin" on MTV Video Music Awards show, her first U.S. Number 1 single by December 1984.
November 1984	Madonna's second studio album, *Like a Virgin*, released.
1985	*Material Girl* video, directed by Mary Lambert. Madonna meets Sean Penn on the set. *Crazy for You* MTV video, directed by Harold Becker. Madonna wins seven *Billboard Music Awards*, including Top Pop Artist.
March 1985	Madonna co-stars with Rosanna Arquette in new film, *Desperately Seeking Susan*, directed by Susan Seidelman, featuring Madonna's song, "Into the Groove." Release of the film *Vision Quest* with Madonna in cameo role singing "Crazy for You."
April 1985	Madonna's first nationwide tour, *Like a Virgin*, kicks off in Seattle.
May 1985	Madonna featured on the cover of *Time* magazine.
August 1985	Madonna and Sean Penn are married on her birthday, August 16, in Malibu, California; the newlyweds buy a house in Malibu and begin married life.
1986	Madonna's third studio album, *True Blue*, released. Controversy erupts over songs and videos of "Papa Don't Preach" and "Open Your Heart."

August 1986	Shanghai Surprise, starring Madonna and Sean Penn, released to negative reviews.
	Madonna and Sean star in short run of David Rabe play, *Goose and Tom-Tom*, at Lincoln Center in New York City.
June 1987	Madonna's *Who's That Girl?* worldwide tour opens in Japan.
July 1987	Sean serves time in California jail for assaulting photographers.
August 1987	*Who's That Girl?* film released, starring Madonna and Griffin Dunne, tepid reviews.
September 1987	Madonna wins Best Female Video for *Papa Don't Preach* at MTV Video Music Awards.
December 1987	Madonna files for divorce from Sean Penn.
1988	Madonna dates John F. Kennedy, Jr., then takes up with comedian Sandra Bernhard.
January 1988	Withdraws divorce papers.
May 1988	Stars in David Mamet play, *Speed-the-Plow*, on Broadway. New York Daily News headline: "No, She Can't Act."
December 1988	Sean arrested for beating up Madonna; she does not press charges.
1989	*Like a Prayer* video wins Viewers Choice at MTV Music Awards.
	Bloodhounds of Broadway released starring Madonna, Matt Dillon, Jennifer Grey, Randy Quaid; negative reviews.
	Madonna is named one of the "25 Most Intriguing People in the World for 1989" by *People* magazine (named again in 1992 and 2001, and as one of the "25 Legends of the 20th Century" in 1999).
January 1989	Madonna files for divorce from Sean again. Divorce finalized at the end of January. Madonna buys new house and moves to Hollywood Hills.
February 1989	Begins filming *Dick Tracy* with Warren Beatty; they become a couple.
March 1989	*Like a Prayer*, Madonna's fourth studio album, released. Pepsi cancels deal to feature Madonna in a major commercial when public controversy over Like a Prayer video erupts.

March 1990   *Vogue* video premieres on MTV. "Vogue"
                  and "Keep It Together" singles released. The
                  "Vogue" single is certified as 2x platinum by
                  June 1989, the biggest selling single by a female
                  artist ever.

April 1990   Madonna's *Blond Ambition* worldwide tour opens.
                  I'm Breathless album of music from film *Dick
                  Tracy* released.

June 1990   Dick Tracy, starring Madonna as Breathless
                  Mahoney, with Warren Beatty, released to
                  favorable reviews.

September 1990   Actor Tony Ward is Madonna's new boyfriend;
                  moves in with her.

October 1990   Madonna appears on MTV for "Rock the Vote,"
                  wrapped in an American flag. Veterans protest.

November 1990   *The Immaculate Collection* greatest hits CD and
                  video released.
                  MTV network executives ban the *Justify My
                  Love* video; "Justify My Love" single is certified
                  platinum by February 1991.

March 1991   Madonna attends 63rd Academy Awards with
                  Michael Jackson, performs "Sooner or Later"
                  from *Dick Tracy*, which wins Oscar for Best Song.

May 1991   *Truth or Dare* documentary of Madonna's *Blond
                  Ambition* tour is released. Madonna goes to
                  Cannes, France for premiere.

February 1992   Madonna wins first Grammy award, Best Video,
                  for *Blond Ambition Tour Live*.
                  Madonna and her bodyguard, Jim Albright,
                  begin two-year relationship during photo
                  shoot for *Sex* book in Florida. Madonna buys
                  $5 million house on Biscayne Bay.

March 1992   Woody Allen's film, *Shadows and Fog*, released
                  with Madonna in cameo role as trapeze artist.

April 1992   Madonna forms Maverick, a record and music
                  publishing company, with Time Warner.

July 1992   *A League of Their Own* by Penny Marshall
                  starring Madonna and Rosie O'Donnell
                  released to favorable reviews. Song, "This Used
                  to Be My Playground" becomes Madonna's
                  10th Number 1 single.

October 1992	"Erotica" single and *Erotica*, her fifth studio album, and video released.
	Madonna's *Sex*, book of erotica released, sells record 150,000 copies on first day, 500,000 copies in one week, Number 1 on *The New York Times* nonfiction bestseller list.
January 1993	Film, *Body of Evidence*, starring Madonna, is released. Her second film that year, *Dangerous Game*, goes straight to video.
September 1993	Madonna's worldwide tour, *The Girlie Show* opens in England. Puerto Rico officials outraged when she pulls a Puerto Rican flag through her crotch.
March 1994	Madonna says the f- word 13 times during her appearance on *The David Letterman Show*.
October 1994	Madonna struts the runway in Paris in Jean-Paul Gaultier's spring/summer 1995 collection.
	Bedtime Stories, Madonna's sixth studio album, released.
January 1995	Madonna named Number 10 on Earl Blackwell's 35th list of the Worst-Dressed Women of 1994.
February 1995	Madonna is signed to star in film *Evita* as Eva Peron.
May 1995	Stalker Robert Hoskins is shot on Madonna's Hollywood Hills property and arrested.
October 1995	*Blue in the Face* film released; Madonna in cameo role.
December 1995	Madonna receives VH1 Most Fashionable Artist award, presented by her ex-husband, Sean Penn.
1996	Begins attending classes at Kabbalah Centre in Los Angeles, California.
January 1996	Trial of Robert Hoskins, stalker of Madonna. She is subpoenaed to testify. He is convicted on five counts of assault and threatening to kill Madonna and sentenced to 10 years in jail.
	Madonna arrives in Buenos Aires, Argentina to begin filming *Evita*. She is greeted with protests and graffiti.
March 1996	*Girl 6* film by Spike Lee released with Madonna in bit part as phone sex company owner.
April 1996	Madonna announces she is three months pregnant by boyfriend Carlos Leon.

October 1996	Gives birth to Lourdes Maria Ciccone Leon in Los Angeles, California.
December 1996	*Evita* is released on Christmas Day to favorable reviews.
1997	Parts with manager Freddy DeMann after 15 years. New manager is Caresse Henry of Q-Prime. Parts with Carlos Leon. New boyfriend is Andy Bird, aspiring British actor and playwright.
January 1997	Lourdes Maria Ciccone is baptized at St. Jude Melkite Catholic Church in Miami, Florida.
January 1997	Madonna named Number 3 on Earl Blackwell's 37th list of Best-Dressed Women.
February 1997	Madonna wins first Golden Globe Award, as Best Actress in a Motion Picture for *Evita*.
January 1998	Madonna opens *Ray of Light* tour in London.
March 1998	*Ray of Light*, Madonna's seventh studio album, released.
May 1998	*Ray of Light* video premieres on MTV.
August 1998	Madonna celebrates her 40th birthday on August 16.
September 1998	Madonna wins five awards including Best Video for *Ray of Light* video at MTV Music Awards.
November 1998	Madonna meets Guy Ritchie at home of Trudy Styler and Sting in England.
February 1999	*Ray of Light* album wins Grammy as Best Pop Album, plus three other Grammy awards.
September 1999	*Beautiful Stranger* video from *Austin Powers 2: The Spy Who Shagged Me* wins Best Video from a Film award at MTV Music Awards.
December 1999	Madonna moves to England, rents house in Notting Hill, London.
March 2000	Announces she is pregnant with her second child. Guy Ritchie is the father. *The Next Best Thing* with Madonna and Rupert Everett released to negative reviews.
June 2000	Madonna is a guest at charity dinner given by Prince Charles at his home in Gloucestershire, England.
August 2000	Madonna gives birth to a son, Rocco John Ritchie, on August 11 in Los Angeles, California. *Music* video premieres on MTV, "Music" single released, Madonna's 12th Number 1 single.

September 2000	*Music*, Madonna's eighth studio album, released, first Number 1 album since *Like a Prayer* in 1989. Nominated for four Grammy Awards (but doesn't win).
December 2000	Madonna and Guy Ritchie announce their engagement and wedding plans. Madonna buys an $8 million house in London.
December 21, 2000	Rocco John Ritchie is christened at Dornoch Cathedral in Dornoch, Scotland.
December 22, 2000	Madonna and Guy Ritchie are married at Skibo Castle, Dornoch, Scotland.
January 2001	Madonna named Number 4 on Earl Blackwell's 41st list of the Worst-Dressed Women of 2000.
June 2001	Begins *Drowned World* worldwide tour in Spain.
September 2001	Donates proceeds from her last tour concert in Los Angeles on September 15 to victims of 9/11 World Trade Center attack.
November 2001	Named Britain's highest-earning woman, with an annual income of $43.8 million.
December 2001	Presented with her own plaid tartan by the Scottish Highland Tourist Board in recognition of her contribution to Scottish tourism and as a wedding present.
May 2002	Opens two-month run in *Up For Grabs*, play by David Williamson in London.
October 2002	Guy Ritchie's film, *Swept Away*, starring Madonna, is released to disappointing reviews.
November 2002	Madonna meets Queen Elizabeth II at the world premiere of James Bond film, *Die Another Day* (in which Madonna makes a cameo appearance as a fencing instructor). Her recording of the theme song, "Die Another Day," becomes her 35th Top 10 hit in the United States, Number 3 in the United Kingdom.
April 2003	Controversy envelops Madonna's *American Life* video because of its war images and critical stance even before it is released: she announces that she will cancel it. Releases "American Life" single and *American Life*, ninth studio album, lowest-selling album of her career.

August 2003	Performs with Britney Spears and Christina Aguilera at MTV Music Video Awards, plants much-discussed kiss on Britney's mouth.
September 2003	Madonna's first children's book, *The English Roses*, is published. Madonna has a tea party to launch it. Book is ranked Number 1 on *The New York Times* best-seller list of children's books by October.
November 2003	Second children's book, *Mr. Peabody's Apples*, is published. Madame Tussaud's Wax Museum in New York City unveils a wax figure model of Madonna.
2004	Madonna's third and fourth children's books are published: *The Adventures of Abdi* and *Yakov and the Seven Thieves*.
June 2004	Madonna begins *Re-Invention* worldwide tour, highest-grossing tour of 2004, earning $125 million.
2005	Madonna's fifth children's book, *Lotsa Casha*, published.
November 2005	*Confessions on a Dance Floor*, Madonna's tenth studio album, released. "Hung Up" single from album hits *Billboard* Hot 100 chart, tying her with Elvis Presley for the most Top 10 songs on the U.S. singles chart.
June 2006	Madonna begins *Confessions on a Dance Floor* worldwide tour. Controversy erupts in Italy, Germany, the Czech Republic, and Russia over her crucifix scene.
June 2006	Madonna's second documentary, *I've Got a Secret to Tell You* filmed during her *Re-Invention* tour in 2004 and directed by Jonas Akerlund, released.
August 2006	Madonna's *Hung Up* video is nominated for five MTV Video Awards: Video of the Year, Best Female Video, Best Dance Video, Best Pop Video, Best Choreography.
October 2006	Madonna and Guy Ritchie adopt a 13-month-old Malawi child, David Banda.
November 2006	NBC broadcasts two-hour *Madonna: The Confessions Tour Live*, taped at London Wembley Arena tour performance.

TIMELINE

Madonna's Studio Albums

1983   *Madonna*
1984   *Like a Virgin*
1986   *True Blue*
1989   *Like a Prayer*
1992   *Erotica*
1994   *Bedtime Stories*
1998   *Ray of Light*
2000   *Music*
2003   *American Life*
2005   *Confessions on a Dance Floor*

Madonna's Number 1 U.S. Singles

1984   "Like a Virgin," "Crazy for You."
1986   "Live to Tell," "Paper Don't Preach," "Open Your Heart."
1987   "Who's That Girl?"
1989   "Like a Prayer."
1990   "Vogue," "Justify My Love."
1992   "This Used to Be My Playground."
1994   "Take a Bow."
2000   "Music."
2005   "Hung Up."

Madonna's Videos

1982   *Everybody*
1983   *Burning Up*
1984   *Borderline*
1984   *Like a Virgin*
1985   *Material Girl*
1985   *Crazy for You*
1985   *Into the Groove*
1985   *Dress You Up*
1985   *Gambler*
1985   *Over and Over*
1986   *Live to Tell*
1986   *Papa Don't Preach*
1986   *Open Your Heart*
1987   *La Isla Bonita*
1987   *Causing a Commotion*

1987	*The Look of Love*
1989	*Like a Prayer*
1989	*Express Yourself*
1989	*Cherish*
1989	*Oh Father*
1990	*Vogue*
1990	*Vote!*
1990	*Justify My Love*
1991	*This Used to Be My Playground*
1992	*Erotica*
1992	*Deeper and Deeper*
1993	*Bad Girl*
1993	*Fever*
1993	*Rain*
1994	*I'll Remember*
1994	*Secret*
1994	*Take a Bow*
1995	*Bedtime Story*
1995	*Human Nature*
1995	*You'll See*
1996	*Love Don't Live Here Anymore*
1996	*You Must Love Me*
1996	*Don't Cry for Me Argentina*
1998	*Frozen*
1998	*Ray of Light*
1998	*The Power of Goodbye*
1999	*Nothing Really Matters*
1999	*Beautiful Stranger*
2000	*AmericanPie*
2000	*Music*
2000	*Don't Tell Me*
2001	*What It Feels Like for a Girl*
2002	*Die Another Day*
2003	*Hollywood*
2003	*American Life*
2003	*Me Against the Music (Britney Spears, featuring Madonna)*
2003	*Love Profusion*
2005	*Hung Up*
2006	*Sorry*
2006	*Get Together*
2006	*Jump*

Madonna's Films

1980	*A Certain Sacrifice*, directed by Stephen Jon Lewicki.
1983	*Vision Quest*, directed by Harold Becker.
1985	*Desperately Seeking Susan*, directed by Susan Seidelman.
1986	*Shanghai Surprise*, directed by Jim Goddard.
1987	*Who's That Girl?*, directed by James Foley.
1989	*Bloodhounds of Broadway*, directed by Howard Brookner.
1990	*Dick Tracy*, directed by Warren Beatty.
1992	*A League of Their Own*, directed by Penny Marshall.
1992	*Shadows and Fog*, directed by Woody Allen.
1993	*Body of Evidence*, directed by Ulrich Edel.
1993	*Dangerous Game*, directed by Abel Ferrara.
1995	*Blue in the Face*, directed by Paul Auster.
1995	*Four Rooms*, directed by Allison Anders.
1996	*Evita*, directed by Alan Parker.
1996	*Girl 6*, directed by Spike Lee.
2000	*The Next Best Thing*, directed by John Schlesinger.
2002	*Swept Away*, directed by Guy Ritchie.

Madonna's Documentaries

1991	*Truth or Dare*, directed by Alek Keshishian.
2006	*I've Got a Secret to Tell You*, directed by Jonas Akerlund.

Plays

1986	*Goose and Tom-Tom* by David Rabe, Lincoln Center, New York.
1988	*Speed-the-Plow* by David Mamet, Royale Theater, Broadway.
2002	*Up for Grabs* by David Williamson, Wyndhams Theatre, London, England.

Information for this chronology was taken from Maurice Gravelle, "Madonna Career Diary," available at www.AbsoluteMadonna.com (accessed August 6, 2006). Also, "Madonna," Wikipedia, available at www.wikipedia.org (accessed August 3, 2006). Finally, Andrew Morton, *Madonna* (New York: St. Martin's Press, 2001).

Chapter 1

MADONNA LOUISE VERONICA CICCONE

Madonna was born on August 16, 1958 at 7:05 A.M. at Mercy Hospital in Bay City, Michigan to Silvio "Tony" Ciccone, a first-generation Italian, and Madonna Louise Firkin, a French Canadian. Baby Madonna was the third child and first girl in the family, and she was named after her mother. That single name, Madonna, the traditional name for the Virgin Mary, would turn out to be her most valuable asset in branding herself as America's top pop icon. It would ultimately also be ironic as a name for a star whose tactics of shock and awe constantly tested the boundaries of female propriety. As she would later say, "I sometimes think I was born to live up to my name. How could I be anything else but what I am having been named Madonna? I would either have ended up a nun or this."[1]

When Madonna was born, Dwight Eisenhower was president for the second time, the Beatles were still warming up in Liverpool, and Elvis Presley was the king of rock and roll. Pop Art, Andy Warhol, and the hippies of the 1960s were just over the horizon. High culture in America was about to be knocked off its pedestal, given an assist by that engine of mass culture, television. Madonna couldn't have been born at a better time.

Three more children were still to come in the Ciccone family, and there were already two at home when Madonna was born, living in the small bungalow at 443 Thor Street in Pontiac, Michigan, a racially mixed suburb about 25 miles northwest of Detroit. Her mother had decided that she wanted her family physician, Dr. Abraham H. Jacoby in Bay City, to deliver this baby, so the Ciccones packed up and went there to await the birth at the home of Elsie Fortin, Madonna Sr.'s mother.[2] Madonna later spent many vacations with this grandmother and came to know her well; Elsie Fortin was one of the few people whose advice she valued.

From all accounts, growing up in the large Ciccone family was busy and happy, and Madonna's childhood, at least until the age of five, was quite normal. She already had two older brothers when she arrived in the family, Anthony ("Little Tony"), 2, born in May 1956, and Martin ("Mard"), 1, born a year later in August, 1957.

Madonna had a nickname, too, "Little Nonnie," to keep the names straight with her mother. Madonna, Sr. seems to have been devoted and loving, taking tender care of her brood. She had three more children after Madonna: Paula, Christopher, and Melanie, and had been pregnant nearly every year of her seven-year marriage.

Madonna's father Tony, was an Old World patriarch at home and the disciplinarian of the family. The children were sent to parochial school, and Tony made sure they went to Mass on Sundays and even on school day mornings. This strong Catholic upbringing left its mark on Madonna who, although she has rebelled against it time after time, was deeply imprinted by her religious background.

DIVA IN TRAINING

Madonna was a pretty little girl, with blue-green eyes and dark brown hair, and a streak of exhibitionism that helped get her the attention she craved even then. She has a slight gap in her front teeth (supposedly a sign of sociability), which was never corrected, although later for her videos and movies she would disguise it. She also has a small mole under her right nostril, sometimes disguised, sometimes emphasized in later photographs. Madonna is short, at 5 feet, 4½ inches, a fact that surprises when one sees this larger-than-life woman in the flesh.

At an early age, Madonna exhibited a diva streak and liked to dance and show off for the grownups at family gatherings. There were many of these gatherings, as both parents came from large families. Her paternal grandparents, Gaetano and Michelina Ciccone, had come from Italy in the 1920s from Pacentro, near Florence in the Abruzzi region northeast of Rome, seeking the better life that so many Italians—more than 27 million between 1880 and 1930—left home to find in America. The Ciccones had been peasant farmers in Italy for generations. Crop failures, World War I, and a flu epidemic now were making life difficult. Gaetano, his aunt and uncle, and a cousin decided to strike out for the new country, boarding a ship in Naples. They settled in Aliquippa, outside of Pittsburgh, Pennsylvania, where Gaetano went to work in the steel mill. His wife, whom he had married in Pacentro, joined him in 1925.[3] The couple raised a family of six boys, including Silvio (Tony), their youngest son and the only one to get a college degree. Madonna saw these grandparents frequently. She remembers that they did not speak any English:

> They lived in a sort of an Italian ghetto-type neighborhood. I think in a way they represented an old lifestyle that my father really didn't want to have anything to do with. It's not that he was ashamed, really, but he wanted to be better. I think he wanted to be upwardly mobile and go into the educated, prosperous America. I think he wanted us to have a better life than he did when he was growing up.[4]

The Fortins, on Madonna's mother's side, had a longer pedigree, with ancestors who came to Canada in the 1650s from France. (Interestingly, Madonna and French-Canadian singer Celine Dion are distantly related way back in the Fortin family tree. Madonna is also related to Gwen Stefani through her Ciccone grandparents.) Some of the Fortin family eventually migrated to the United States, and Madonna's maternal grandparents, Willard and Elsie Fortin, settled in Bay City, Michigan, where they raised eight children, including Madonna's mother. Tony Ciccone met his future wife when she was just 17, at a wedding he attended while serving in the Air Force in Texas. She was, by all accounts, a beauty, and four years later, in 1955, they were married in Bay City. Tony had just graduated from Geneva College as a physics major, and had taken a job as an optics and defense engineer for the Chrysler Corporation (later, General Dynamics) that was to be his lifelong career. They moved to Pontiac, Michigan, where the family would live until Madonna was 10 years old.

The house in Pontiac wasn't really big enough for all these children, and Madonna had to share a bedroom with her two little sisters. Naturally, there was a lot of competition for attention in a large family and Madonna learned early on how to get it, sometimes by being a goody-two shoes, sometimes by being outrageous. Her older brothers, Little Tony and Mard, liked to tease her; once, according to a family story, they hung Madonna up on a clothesline by her blouse, leaving her marooned until her stepmother plucked her down.

A DEATH IN THE FAMILY

In 1962, when Madonna was four, her mother, pregnant with Melanie, developed breast cancer. Madonna Sr. did not seek treatment until she had weaned the new baby,[5] but by then it was too late. She spent the last year of her life in Bay City's Mercy Hospital undergoing chemotherapy. Madonna and her brothers and sisters were taken regularly to visit her. By the first of December in 1963, Madonna's mother was dead. She was only 31 years old. Madonna was only 5½. The family blamed her death on a part-time job she had had as an x-ray technician in the days before lead aprons were required equipment.

For any young girl, the death of her mother is a traumatic event. For Madonna, it has been *the* event of her entire life. She has never forgotten nor, it would seem, ever been reconciled to her mother's early death. In her own words, she feels "gypped."[6] Child psychologists say that a girl who loses her mother at such an early age is indeed deprived of important development in the oedipal period, when a close connection with her mother helps her work through her natural attachment to her father.[7] Madonna's ongoing and obsessive love-hate relationship with her father may be the result of those unresolved issues. She has wrestled with some of these issues in her songs and videos, particularly in the *Oh Father* video, where her father is shown as a dark presence and she is shown visiting her mother's grave with him.

Madonna wrote about her memories of her mother in the diary she kept much later during the filming of *Evita*, remembering the religious rituals of Eastertide when her mother, a very observant Catholic, covered up "all the religious pictures and statues in the house with purple cloth." In the diary, Madonna thinks about "how my mother must have felt with my father when he told her she was dying. And how she stayed so cheerful and never gave in to her sadness even at the end."[8] On Mother's Day that year (1996), Madonna was pregnant herself, and wrote, "I long to know the sensation of having a mother to hug or call up and say conspiratorial things to about how difficult men are, or simply share my joy with. This year I am even sadder because I'm sure she would be the happiest to know that I am having a baby."[9]

In a 1985 interview with *Time* magazine, Madonna recalls her mother as "a very forgiving and angelic person," someone who didn't yell even though "we were really messy, awful kids."

> I remember also I knew she was sick for a long time with breast cancer. . . . I know she tried to keep her feelings inside, her fear inside, and not let us know. She never complained. I remember she was really sick and was sitting on the couch. I went up to her and I remember climbing on her back and saying, "Play with me, play with me," and she wouldn't. She couldn't and she started crying and I got really angry with her and I remember,

like, pounding her back with my fist and saying, "Why are you doing this?" Then I realized she was crying. . . . I was so little and I put my arms around her and I could feel her body underneath me sobbing and I felt like she was the child. . . . That was the turning point when I knew.[10]

Madonna said that realizing her mother was so sick made her grow up quickly. "I knew I could be either sad and weak and not in control or I could just take control and say it's going to get better."[11] Control issues became paramount for Madonna after her mother died. There was so much about her young life that she couldn't control that it became an obsession with her to take charge, a behavior pattern that frequently brought her smack up against her father and stepmother, and later, everyone else. She began to use rebellion and outrage to get her way.

Everything turned upside down in the Ciccone household when Madonna's mother died. Suddenly, Madonna herself had to be a mother to her younger siblings and help take care of the house. "I feel like all my adolescence was spent taking care of babies and changing diapers and baby-sitting," she told *Time* magazine in 1985. "I have to say I resented it, because when all my friends were out playing, I felt like I had all these adult responsibilities. I think that's when I really thought about how I wanted to do something else and get away from all that."[12] Her father went through a succession of housekeepers in the next three years, and Madonna and her siblings were frequently farmed out to relatives. The children all reacted differently to their mother's death. The older boys became difficult to handle; Madonna had nightmares and refused to leave the house except to go to school. Being with her little kindergarten friends there at least gave her some sense of normality.

OH FATHER

Her kindergarten teacher at St. Frederick's school in Pontiac, writing a note to the nun who would be Madonna's first-grade teacher, observed, "12/1/63 Mother died. Needs a great deal of love and attention."[13] In school, Madonna found another way to get noticed at home, by getting good grades. Her father would give his children 50 cents for As on their report cards and Madonna, who has an unusually high IQ over 140, found it easy to become a straight A student.[14] She played up to her father in this and every other way she could, wanting to be the apple of his eye. "I was my father's favorite," she said later. "I knew how to wrap him around my finger. . . . I was really competitive, and my brothers and sisters hated me for it. I made the most money off of every report card."[15]

In 1966, someone else caught Tony's eye. Blonde Joan Gustafson came into the household as a housekeeper, and six months later, she married Madonna's father. Feeling betrayed and angry, and refusing her father's request to call Joan "Mom," Madonna at age eight turned from being a conforming little good girl into a difficult child, getting attention by being a rebel. This worked so well to channel her anger and attract the kind of attention she would always crave that, even as an adult, she continued to use outrage and rebellion as methods of getting noticed. This strategy, in fact, became the *modus operandi* that helped propel her later career to the top of the charts.

Madonna continued to excel at school, but she began to test the limits of parental control elsewhere in every direction. "I remember always being told to shut up," she told a *Time* magazine reporter later.[16] "Everywhere, at home, at school, I always got in trouble for talking out of turn. I got tape over my mouth. I got my mouth washed out with soap. Everything. Mouthing off comes naturally."[17] But the nuns were strict at the Catholic school (St. Andrew's in Rochester Hills) Madonna attended until she was 12 years old. At one point, Madonna even thought she wanted to be a nun. For her confirmation when she was nine, she chose the name of Veronica, attracted to the story of the saint wiping the brow of Jesus on his way to crucifixion. But Madonna was also good at taunting the nuns who were her teachers and once, with a girlfriend, she spied on them after dark (her big discovery was that nuns had hair on their heads under their white wimples).[18]

Madonna seems always to have had plenty of friends in elementary school. Growing up, she played with Barbie dolls and listened to Motown records with her friends and joined the Camp Fire Girls. Madonna was a popular girl in high school, too, but distinguished herself as a nonconformist, refusing to shave under her arms, mouthing off to her teachers, and acquiring a reputation as "fast," most of it an act. Two of her girlfriends at the time, Ruth Dupack and Carol Belanger, say they also heard plenty from Madonna about her dislike of her stepmother and the disputes she had with her over clothing and behavior.[19] At slumber parties, the friends discussed boys and sex, and Madonna later claimed that that was how she learned about sexuality and other matters, like how to use a tampon. As close as they were at the time, Madonna doesn't seem to have kept up with these girlhood friends, however, and when one, Moira McPharlin, came to see her years later during her *Blond Ambition* tour, Madonna seems to have shrugged her off rather cruelly.[20] Once she moved out of the Midwest, Madonna apparently didn't want to look back.

CINDERELLA AND HER STEPMOTHER

Meanwhile, Tony and Joan had two more children, Jennifer, born in 1967, and Mario, born in 1968. Their family of eight children was bursting out of the bungalow in Pontiac. They had to find a bigger house, and in 1968 they moved to Rochester Hills, a more upscale suburb north of Detroit. Unlike the scruffier town of Pontiac, Rochester was a solidly middle-class, all white community. Madonna would later claim she grew up in a working-class town and played with the black kids, which, in the first 10 years of her life, she probably did. But Rochester Hills and the red brick and clapboard colonial house at 2036 Oklahoma Street she lived in until she graduated from the public high school didn't quite fit the picture of the hardscrabble childhood she would later paint. Her father's successful career at Chrysler gave him the means to support his large family comfortably. As patriarchal and undemonstrative as he was, Tony was a good father to his children and taught them a code of moral and religious behavior by living it himself. He set the standards that Madonna would gleefully, if guiltily, flout.

> My father was very strong. I don't agree with some of his values but he did have integrity, and if he told us not to do something he didn't do it either. He believed that making love to someone is a very sacred thing and it shouldn't happen until after you are married. He stuck by those beliefs, and that represented a very strong person to me. He was my role model.[21]

Yet without a mother, a female role model to emulate, Madonna seems to have chosen to rebel against her father's standards. "I didn't have a mother, like maybe a female role model, and I was left on my own a lot, and I think that probably gave me courage to do things."[22]

Certainly her father's remarriage and the presence of the stepmother she viewed as an interloper continued to gnaw at Madonna. Indeed, it seems that she has never fully resolved her feelings toward her stepmother, who, when Madonna was growing up, was something of a disciplinarian. Madonna's outward defiance of her stepmother brought her swift punishment, however.

Madonna discovered that fashion offered her a good way to fight back; she refused to wear the identical outfits her stepmother chose for all the girls and deliberately wore mismatched socks and clothes. Madonna would leave for school wearing one set of clothes and change into another when she got there. Joan said she was worried that Madonna would grow up to be a "floozy."[23]

It was a bitter pill for all the children when Joan, at Tony's urging, formally adopted them in 1969. At the family party celebrating the adoption, Madonna threw up (she admits to having a "weak stomach" and often reacted this way to upsetting events and stress). The adoption seemed to definitely confirm that her mother was dead and never coming back. Perhaps Madonna viewed herself as a kind of Cinderella in the situation, with Joan as the wicked stepmother. The most hurtful part was that she felt she had lost some of her father's affection when he remarried. She was learning, in a rather fierce and bitter way, to rely on no one but herself. And Madonna had the supreme self-confidence and strong will to do it. These have been major assets in her climb to success through many setbacks. She has, in addition, been careful never to let herself fall prey to the drugs and alcohol so rampant in the music industry, and does not smoke. "I don't take drugs," Madonna says. "I never did. They don't do anything for me. All the feelings I think drugs are supposed to produce in you, confidence or energy, I can produce naturally in my body."[24] As she announced in her documentary, *Truth or Dare*, she is more "interested in pushing people's buttons and being provocative," a strategy she had found attention-getting even when she was growing up.[25]

BAD GIRL

Sex, she discovered early on, was the best way to be provocative. Even at West Junior High in Rochester Hills, Madonna started to garner a reputation as a "fast" girl, although it was essentially all an act then. "If I liked a boy, I'd confront him," she told *Time* magazine about her tactics. "I've always been that way. Maybe it comes from having older brothers and sharing the bathroom with them or whatever. But when you're that aggressive in junior high, the boys get the wrong impression of you."[26] She had always been a flirt, and she learned to use it to her advantage, enjoying the tease and the attention she got from boys. Her stepmother's explanation of sex seemed to leave out all the good parts, and Madonna says she learned the most about sex when she was growing up from her girlfriends. By the time she was 15, however, she decided she needed to test out what she knew on a member of the opposite sex. She asked her then boyfriend, Russell Long, one of the school's athletes who was two years older, to introduce her to sex. He obliged in the backseat of his father's car.[27] As she was rumored to have since had affairs with the likes of artist Jean-Michel Basquiat and John Kennedy Jr., as well as Warren Beatty and other luminaries, this was an inauspicious sexual beginning for Madonna. Later, she would call losing her virginity a "career move."[28]

At Rochester Adams High in the early 1970s, Madonna distinguished herself as a boy-crazy, fun-loving girl even as she maintained her all-A average. She joined the cheerleading squad and was good at the acrobatics required, although the flesh-colored tights she wore were intended to shock—and did. She also helped start a thespian club to put on plays and musicals in which Madonna usually had a leading role, including that of Eliza Doolittle in *My Fair Lady*. "When there was a role for, like, a forward, bad girl, everybody sort of unanimously looked over at me when they were casting it," she commented later.[29] She had already managed to outrage her father with a performance in a school talent show when she was 13, flashing the audience in a revealing body suit she wore under a trench coat. And she had already made her film debut in a 1976 video made by one of her classmates in which an egg is shown "frying" on Madonna's yet-to-be-famous belly button (Madonna would probably not be pleased to know that this 1976 one-minute video is now posted on the *ifilm* website's "Viral Videos" section). She commented on this in an interview with *Time* magazine in 1985:

> Yeah, well, I do like my belly button. They [keep] talking about my cute belly button. I think there are other unobvious places on the body that are sexy and the stomach is kind of innocent. I don't have a really flat stomach. I sort of have a little girl's stomach. It's round and the skin is smooth and it's nice. I like it.[30]

Acting and showing off came naturally to Madonna. Since childhood she had always loved being the center of attention. Perhaps being the middle child in a big family predisposed her to such tactics. She seemed to be always "on stage" anyway, coyly acting out the various roles she happened to be playing for the moment in her everyday life. Madonna admired Hollywood stars like Marlene Dietrich, Judy Holliday, Marilyn Monroe, Carole Lombard, and even Shirley Temple, and later Madonna would imitate Dietrich and Monroe in her videos. When she was little, Madonna said she wanted to be either a movie star or a nun. Hollywood always had a glamorous allure for her and two of the major men in her life, Sean Penn, whom she married, and Warren Beatty, were movie stars. Madonna felt that she herself did have acting talent and, throughout her music career, she constantly pursued roles in film and the theater. She has been in 14 films, either in a leading role or a cameo part, and 3 plays. But in only three of these—*Desperately Seeking Susan, Dick Tracy,* and *Evita*—did Madonna receive critical accolades. As good as she could be in a three-minute video, she could not seem to be able to portray a fully fleshed-out character unless it was some version of herself. As Michael Musto, a critic for the *Village Voice,* said, "She is too aware of the camera and trying to look good. Too aware of herself."[31] Self-conscious, in other words. As Warren Beatty would remark later in the *Truth or Dare* documentary, she loves the camera: "She doesn't want to *live* off camera."[32]

DANCING QUEEN

Meanwhile, Madonna's father was trying to channel his daughter's talent for attention-seeking in a more productive way. He wanted her to take piano lessons, which she tried, hated, and ultimately just wasn't very good at. Music was definitely on her agenda, but the piano wasn't. Growing up, she naturally listened to a lot of Motown music, which originated in Detroit, and she admired Nancy Sinatra, especially her song, "These Boots Are Made for Walking," which appealed to Madonna's need to boss people around. "Yeah," Madonna said later. "Give me some of those go-go boots. I want to walk on a few people."[33] She could picture herself as a star like Nancy Sinatra or Diana Ross of the Supremes. It just wasn't clear yet how she was going to get there.

Madonna had a friend who was taking ballet lessons and she talked her father into letting her take ballet instead of piano. Madonna, at 15, soon distinguished herself in dance, starting herself on a path that would lead to a scholarship to the University of Michigan. At the Rochester School of Ballet, the owner/instructor, Christopher Flynn, recognized Madonna as having the talent to be an excellent dancer, and he took a special interest in helping her succeed. She was lithe and agile and had the discipline and commitment to do well. Avowedly gay, Flynn took her out with him to the gay nightclubs in downtown Detroit, where they often stole the show on the dance floor together, doing the latest dance steps. Dance lessons suddenly opened up a career path that Madonna was passionate about. And Christopher Flynn was going to make sure that doors opened for her. Madonna credits him with giving her the courage to eventually go to New York.

In Madonna's senior year, Flynn had taken a position teaching dance at the University of Michigan in Ann Arbor, and he helped convince the university dance department chairman that his protégée, Madonna, was worthy of a scholarship. To her father's great satisfaction, Madonna won the scholarship and, upon graduation from high school, enrolled at the University of Michigan. She had just turned 18.

The University of Michigan, often called the Harvard of the Midwest, was a huge Big 10 school in 1976, with an enrollment of more than 20,000 students when Madonna was a freshman. The university and the town of Ann Arbor offered a far more sophisticated environment than Madonna was used to in her relatively sheltered life some 60 miles away in Rochester Hills, with a multicultural student body and an emerging gay and underground scene, sparked with student protests staged on the "Diag," a wide plaza in the middle of the campus. Madonna preferred the off-campus scene and took to it quickly, hanging out in clubs like the Blue Frogge where a black drummer, Steve Bray, attracted her attention and became her boyfriend. He would be a loyal friend and supporter of Madonna's career for a long time afterwards.

Even as a dance major, Madonna had to take the group of courses required for all students, including Freshman English. She had long had an interest in poetry and at college discovered Anne Sexton whose poetry seemed to speak directly to her about her mother's death. Later, living in New York, she read poet Sylvia Plath's *The Bell Jar* about her own experience of setting out for the big city. Other writers she discovered in college were Ernest Hemingway and F. Scott Fitzgerald as well as James Joyce, J. D. Salinger, and Jack Kerouac. During her first year at Michigan, she spent a lot of time alone in her room just reading,[34] and she would continue this pattern. Alone in New York, she carried a book everywhere, even to clubs, because she hated "wasting time," as she told *Rolling Stone* magazine.[35] Today, on tour, she still packs books to read before she goes to sleep at night; on her *Re-Invention* tour, documented in *I've Got a Secret to Tell You*, she is shown reading *Gone With the Wind* and the book of Zohar, the Kabbalah text.

But in her days at the university, the dance curriculum did not allow Madonna much leisure to explore other academic avenues, with two 90-minute technique classes a day plus rehearsals for college performances.[36] Her talent and commitment definitely attracted attention; her ambition and drive made her a totally focused student. She seemed to have a sense that she was destined for bigger things. Some of her classmates recall that, unlike the other students dressed in ballet outfits, Madonna showed up for class wearing torn tights held together with safety pins and cultivated that deliberate *deshabille* she would come to be known for later. Madonna's circle of friends included her second-year roommate, Whitley Setrakian, as well as dance majors Linda Alaniz and Janice Galloway,[37] all of whom she seems to have kept up with when she left the university for New York. Her classmates also noticed that Madonna wanted to please her teacher, Christopher Flynn, who was very strict with his students about their weight. If they veered from 110 to 115 pounds at their weekly weigh-in, he would insist on a diet. Madonna was probably close to being anorexic under this regimen, living off ice cream sundaes and popcorn,[38] but interestingly enough, her weight has stayed in this range ever since.

While Madonna was at the university, she got a chance to audition for a workshop at Alvin Ailey's Dance Studio in New York City, where she was accepted. This was Madonna's first trip to the big city, 600 miles away, and the six weeks she spent there with other aspiring young dancers whetted her appetite for more. Later, back on campus, she got to study with one of Martha Graham's star dancers, Pearl Lang, who was visiting the university as artist-in-residence. These experiences seem to have given new focus to her plans for a dance career. She announced that she was giving up her scholarship and leaving the University of Michigan, after just a year and a half, and going to New York to be a dancer. Christopher Flynn encouraged her to do it. Her father, Tony, was livid. Himself a college graduate, he believed strongly in the value of education and had been proud that one of his children was going to have a college degree. He felt so strongly about it that he told Madonna she'd no longer be his daughter if she left the university.

She did it anyway. At the age of 19, Madonna bought a one-way ticket and flew to New York City, on her first airplane ride ever, where she arrived on a hot day in July 1978, wearing her winter coat and lugging her few belongings. She did not know a soul in the city.

NOTES

1. Quoted by Lynn Hirschberg. "The Misfit." *Vanity Fair*. April 1991. 200.

2. Barbara Victor, *Goddess*. (New York: Cliff Street Books/HarperCollins, 2001), 94.

3. Andrew Morton. *Madonna*. (New York: St. Martin's Press, 2001), 32–34.

4. Quoted by Denise Worrell. "Now: Madonna on Madonna." *Time*, May 27, 1985. www.time.com (accessed August 19, 2006).

5. Victor, 76.

6. Morton, 49.

7. Dr. Claude Delay Tubiana, quoted in Victor, 90–91.

8. "Madonna's Private Diaries," *Vanity Fair*, November 1996. 227.

9. Ibid., 230.

10. Quoted by Worrell. *Time*, May 27, 1985.

11. *Ibid.*

12. *Ibid.*

13. Morton, 51.

14. *Ibid.*, 55.

15. Quoted by Worrell. *Time,*. May 27, 1985.

16. *Ibid.*

17. *Ibid.*

18. J. Randy Taraborrelli. *Madonna:"An Intimate Biography.* (New York: Berkley Books/Simon & Schuster, 2001). 22.

19. Morton, 62.

20. Madonna. *Truth or Dare.* Directed by Alek Keshishian. Miramax, 1990.

21. Quoted by Worrell. *Time,* May 27, 1985.

22. Maureen Orth. "Madonna in Wonderland." *Vanity Fair.* October 1992. 306.

23. Morton, 63.

24. Quoted by Worrell, *Time,* May 27, 1985.

25. *Truth or Dare.* Directed by Alek Keshishian. Miramax, 1990.

26. Quoted by Worrell. *Time,* May 27, 1985.

27. Morton, 69.

28. Quoted by Jay Cocks. "These Big Girls Don't Cry. *Time,* March 4, 1985. www.time.com. (accessed August 10, 2006).

29. Quoted by Worrell, *Time,* May 27, 1985.

30. *Ibid.*

31. Morton, 204.

32. *Truth or Dare.* Directed by Alek Keshishian. Miramax, 1990.

33. Quoted by Worrell, *Time,* May 27, 1985.

34. Victor, xviii; 172.

35. Neil Strauss. "How Madonna Got Her Groove Back." *Rolling Stone.* December 1, 2006, 76.

36. Morton, 80.

37. *Ibid.*, 83.

38. *Ibid.*, 80.

Chapter 2

DESPERATELY SEEKING
STARDOM

"I knew I was going to suffer. I knew it was going to be hard," she later told Ingrid Sischy of *Interview* magazine about her decision to go to New York. "But I was not going back and that's how it was, period."[1] Or, as she would say later in her *Truth or Dare* documentary, "I went to Noo Yawk. I din know anybody."[2]

Madonna instructed the cab driver who brought her into New York City from LaGuardia Airport to drop her off in "the center of everything." He let her out in Times Square, then a honky-tonk part of the city rife with porn shops and peep shows. Dragging her suitcase and sweating in her winter coat, Madonna attracted the attention of a passerby who, in their conversation, found out she had nowhere to live and offered to let her camp out at his apartment. The Good Samaritan was Lionel Bishop, a 33-year-old dancer who lived in Manhattan Towers on Tenth Avenue and 42nd Street, home to many other performers and actors.[3]

Madonna was lucky. This risky arrangement with a stranger could have turned out much differently. As Bishop recalls it, "She approached me. Asked if I knew where she could rent a cheap room and then plowed right ahead asking a million questions about New York. There was just something about her. She was adorable and really ballsy."[4]

Madonna did stay with Bishop until she found her own apartment two weeks later on the Lower East Side, a fourth-floor walk-up at 232 East Fourth Street. It was a bad neighborhood and the apartment was a dump. Madonna later claimed that she had arrived in New York with only $35 in her pocket, one of several legends that have grown up around this story. But "even Madonna wasn't ballsy enough to arrive in New York with just thirty-five dollars," one of her Michigan classmates, Linda Alaniz, later said.[5] Madonna had actually been saving up and stashing away money for this trip, working at a Baskin-Robbins in Ann Arbor.

The New York Madonna came to in 1978 was still recovering from bankruptcy and a massive, crippling blackout the preceding summer. The Son of Sam serial killings had paralyzed the population and the city was suffering a general malaise that the newly elected mayor, Ed Koch, vowed to remedy. It was a dangerous city, rife with crime and homelessness. Gay liberation was well underway after the Stonewall riots and something called AIDS was just beginning to make inroads on that population. A lot of what was happening was still underground, like the burgeoning downtown club scene populated with the soon-to-be famous musicians and artists, party animals, and drugs that Jay McInerny's 1980s novel, *Bright Lights, Big City*, would chronicle. Studio 54 uptown and the Mudd Club downtown were the hot spots. Disco and Donna Summer reigned. *Saturday Night Live* with John Belushi and Bill Murray was just getting started, Archie Bunker was spouting off on TV in *All In the Family*, and Andy Warhol was already famous for his Campbell's soup cans. Women's liberation was bringing housewives into the workplace and generating a backlash, fashion was getting to be more about attitude than hemlines, and sexual adventure was the order of the day. Plunging into this city and this milieu, Madonna was little Miss Middle America, straight out of the suburbs and filled with the longing that still brings the young out of the cornfields and small towns to seek their fortune in New York City. She would have to be a fast learner, and she would have to be tough. She proved to be both.

In Manhattan, Madonna found herself several part-time jobs, none of which lasted very long. She worked for a short time at Dunkin Donuts uptown on West 57th Street until she squirted filling all over a customer and got fired. Later, for $4.50 an hour, she worked as a coat check girl at the Russian Tea Room, also on 57th Street, also until she got fired. Meanwhile, she was looking for work as a dancer. In November that year, she was able to audition for Pearl Lang's Dance Company and was accepted, eventually becoming an assistant to Lang,[6] who said she realized Madonna had something special and was a talented dancer. But things ended in a confrontation when Madonna blew up at her over a dance routine and announced, "I'm going to be a rock star,"[7] even though to that point, she hadn't sung a note. Madonna then got herself accepted for a short workshop with the Alvin Ailey Dance Company, but when it was over, she had to go back to work, this time at a fast-food joint. It was clear that breaking into the dance world in the big city was going to be much tougher than she thought and the competition even tougher.

SURVIVAL TACTICS

Madonna claims she existed during this hard time on popcorn, donuts, and yogurt, with forays into dumpsters for whatever she could scrounge. While this may be part of the legend she has since embroidered about her start in New York, she certainly was up against it during that first winter. Her father came to visit but was so upset by her living conditions—"a roach motel" he called it—that he pleaded with her to come home. He took her out that night to an Italian restaurant for spaghetti, and she wolfed it down.[8] While she lived on the Lower East Side, she was accosted one night by a would-be rapist who forced her at knifepoint to the roof of the building and made her perform oral sex on him. Luckily, Madonna escaped, although she never forgot the fear and feeling of violation she experienced, reenacting the scene in a later movie, *Dangerous Game*, in a hauntingly realistic way.[9]

To earn money that winter, Madonna began posing in the nude for art classes at the Art Students' League in New York. It was familiar work, as she had done some of the same kind of modeling for the art department in Ann Arbor. The pay was only $7 an hour, but the contacts she made there led her to similar work for professional "art" photographers Bill Stone and Martin Schreiber.[10]

Like Marilyn Monroe before her, however, she was going to find out that these nude photographs would resurface later in her career and be an embarrassment to her as a now-famous pop star. The photographs did reappear in 1985 in both *Playboy* and *Penthouse* magazines, and Madonna issued a statement through her publicist, Liz Rosenberg, to say that she was not ashamed of anything. Maybe not; certainly she couldn't have bought the attention and publicity these photographs generated.

Madonna made it through the winter and into the spring of 1979 in a kind of random fashion, living with friends, hanging out with graffiti artists and carrying magic markers to leave her graffiti tag, "Boy Toy" (later to be a slogan on her belt), on sidewalks and subways. Sporadically, she took dance lessons, but, realizing how long it was going to take her to break into the intensely competitive dance world, she started looking around for another way to use her talents. She auditioned for singing as well as dancing parts in television shows and films (she tried out for, but did not make the cut for, the film, *Footloose*, and the TV series, *Fame*). Finally, an audition with two Belgian television producers, Jean van Lieu and Jean-Claude Pellerin, managers of European disco star Patrick Hernandez, landed her a part as a back-up dancer for the star's new cabaret act in Paris, where she would fill in also as a singer. By the end of May 1979, less than a year after she'd arrived in New York City, Madonna was on her way to Paris.

THE FRENCH CONNECTION

Managers Lieu and Pellerin said they could tell Madonna had star potential and in Paris, they began grooming her for bigger parts, getting her a vocal coach (they envisioned her as a singer, perhaps a new Edith Piaf),[11] putting her up in Pellerin's chic 16th arrondissement apartment, buying her clothes, and squiring her around to fancy restaurants and clubs like Regine's. There, on the Rue de Courcelles within walking distance of the lovely Parc Monceau, Madonna lived in aristocratic elegance on the fourth floor of a magnificent nineteenth-century mansion.[12] Her managers signed her up for French lessons and she kept up her dance exercises, but she didn't really have a lot to do as she waited around for something to happen with her new "career." She began spending a lot of time at the Paris flea markets in Montreuil and Montmarte, picking up quirky pieces of clothing and jewelry for her odd outfits. Madonna never did learn to speak much French and she felt isolated and bored in the cocoon the Belgians kept her in. Although she did accompany Hernandez to Tunisia for a photo shoot, it seemed nothing was really happening to launch her on a career path. Despite all the glamour of being in Paris and living a more comfortable life, Madonna was restless and unhappy. Characteristically, she began rebelling, hanging out with street kids around the rough area of the Gare du Nord in Paris, and embarrassing her managers. Finally, she asked them to let her go home to America for a while. She said she'd be back in two weeks, and they agreed.

Once Madonna got back to New York that July, she wired Lieu and Pellerin that she was not coming back to Paris. She had hated it there, yet there was nothing for her in New York. Her 21st birthday was just days away, her hopes for a dance career seemed to have reached a dead end, and after a year of searching, there seemed to be no clear way to satisfy her hunger for success in the New York City music world. Madonna had come to one of several bottoming-out phases she would encounter in her quest for fame and fortune. It would eventually be a turning point, but for now, things looked bleak. An observer has to wonder how Madonna kept going, alone and without resources in a big city that so far had been hostile and unforgiving. It speaks of her intense ambition, drive, and resourcefulness that she didn't pack up and go home to Michigan.

APPRENTICESHIP

Not knowing what else to do, she moved in with Dan Gilroy, a musician she had met and dated before she went to Paris. Picking up where she left off, Madonna stayed with Dan and his brother Ed for a year at their studio in the basement of a Queens synagogue. The brothers, who had full-time jobs, also did gigs as "Bill and Gil" in downtown Manhattan clubs and various other venues. While she lived with them, Madonna learned to play drums and guitar under Dan's tutelage. She also discovered that she could write music, a new dimension of her talents. She wrote a number of songs, most of them now lost, unfortunately. Her sense of rhythm, already well developed from her dance experience, showed in the music of these early songs, which were very danceable and upbeat, according to one biographer who managed to hear the fading tapes. Romantic and angst-filled, they reflected her feelings of loss and longing.[13] Indeed, self-revelation has been a trademark of her music and lyrics, expressing her emotional state and bits of her own experience, as if she is composing a kind of musical autobiography (many of her fans later said that what they like about Madonna's music is that "she tells a story").

Meanwhile, Madonna, always on the lookout for a new direction, had answered an ad to appear in a movie that a New York University film student, Stephen John Lewicki, was planning to make. He liked her off-beat manner and looks and chose her to play Bruna, the dominatrix heroine of his film, titled *A Certain Sacrifice*. All of 60 minutes long and filmed in Washington Square, the movie was really just a student project, but it gave Madonna her first real taste of filmmaking and it would not be her last.[14] She had wanted to be a movie star ever since she was little, and she persevered in this dream for years, despite the mostly negative reviews she would receive for the films she made. This first movie, *A Certain Sacrifice*, was never released; but later, in 1985, Lewicki tried to cash in on Madonna's fame by selling it on video. Madonna offered him $10,000 to withdraw the videos and he turned her down, a decision that made him rich and gave Madonna even more publicity.[15]

She was to spend most of 1980 with Dan and Ed Gilroy, and it would turn out to be an important creative apprenticeship for Madonna, sending her in a new direction and expanding her talents as a musician and singer. Spending her days in the basement of an outer-borough synagogue learning to play drums and guitar was a far cry from her visions of success as a dancer, but whether she realized it or not, Madonna was in fact laying the groundwork for something much bigger. She continued to take dance lessons and to practice with the discipline of a professional, an exercise regimen she had begun under the tutelage of Christopher Flynn and never relinquished. Her daily runs and workouts continued throughout the ups and downs of her quest for stardom. Now, however, intrigued with the discovery of her ability to write songs and play an instrument, she was moving on from dance in a direction that would prove much more fruitful.

MADONNA ON VOCALS

By the end of the summer of 1980, she and the Gilroy brothers had formed their own band, "The Breakfast Club." The name came from the band's habit of practicing all night and then going out for breakfast at a nearby I-Hop. With Madonna on drums and a downtown friend of hers, Angie Smit, on bass guitar, the quartet played their first live gig at the now-defunct downtown UK club in Manhattan.[16] Madonna was thrilled with the performance and began calling all around town to dig up more engagements. They landed one at CBGB (Country Bluegrass Blues), a club on the Lower East Side where more famous groups like Blondie and the Talking Heads played. Taking the mike for a couple of songs, Madonna discovered how much she loved being in front of an audience. She was hungry for more.

As Madonna tried to hog more and more of the show, upstaging Dan and Ed, conflicts among the band members developed. She was also jealous of Angie, whose tendency to wear revealing outfits attracted too much attention and competed with Madonna's own rag-tag ensembles. When another bass guitarist, Gary Burke, showed up in town looking for work, the band decided to hire him and say goodbye to Angie. A friend of the Gilroys, Mike Monahan, also joined the band to play drums.[17] Now Madonna, no longer on the drums, could be front and center as the group's one female member and lead singer. Her idols at the time were Debbie Harry of Blondie and Chrissie Hynde of The Pretenders whom she imitated; yet for someone who had never had any vocal training, let alone sung a song in front of an audience, Madonna was rapidly developing her own style. And if her voice was thin and untrained, she made up for it in attitude and attention-getting antics.

Despite these events, Madonna was getting restless. Encouraged by a record scout who spotted her at one of the band's performances, she decided to leave The Breakfast Club and, with Mike and Gary, start her own band. The breakup with the Gilroys was difficult, yet they seemed to have remained friends with Madonna and were back in a band with her by the end of the year. Madonna moved in with Mike in Douglaston on Long Island and rehearsals for the new group, now called "Madonna and the Sky," got underway in a garage. When the neighbors started to complain about all the noise in the quiet neighborhood, the group found rehearsal space in the Music Building on 39th Street in Manhattan, a dingy building near the Port Authority where other small bands and singers (including at one point, Billy Idol) also practiced.

The band had played only one gig when Mike, who now had a full-time job and a fiancé, announced he could not continue with the group. Undaunted, Madonna called up her ex-boyfriend, drummer Steve Bray, in Ann Arbor, who readily agreed to come to New York and he joined the band in November 1980. It was an important reconnection for both of them. Bray would collaborate with Madonna on writing and producing some of her biggest hits, including "Express Yourself," "Into the Groove," and "Papa Don't Preach." With Madonna, he recorded the four new songs for her first demo tape in August 1981, including "Everybody" and "Burning Up," both written by Madonna. After Madonna became famous, Steve Bray issued a *Pre-Madonna* album of this demo tape. Another collection of early Madonna are some songs she did in 1981 as backup singer for avant-garde German artist Otto von Wernherr, who repackaged them later as *Madonna (& Otto Wernher) In the Beginning*. Apparently Madonna just needed to make a few bucks at the time, and the tracks are said to be "horrific."[18]

The newly formed band, now with Steve Bray, Gary Burke, and a new member, Brian Syms, who had traded them rehearsal space in the Music Building for a place in the band playing lead guitar, was now called "The Millionaires." Then, when the two Gilroy brothers rejoined the band, the group called themselves "Emmy," another of Madonna's many nicknames. Typically, she actually wanted to call the band "Madonna," but the band members squelched that as "too Catholic." They made a demo tape, featuring their rock and roll sound, and managed to get their first booking at the Botany Talk House just before Christmas. Madonna went home to Rochester Hills for the holiday, a respite from her hardscrabble existence certainly, but maybe just a chance to catch her breath and touch base. She was hardly ready to give up yet, but back in New York it was going to be a long, cold winter. By now, Madonna was living in a dirty loft around the corner from the Music Building, just one more temporary abode in her transient existence.

CAUSING A COMMOTION

She had to be questioning the direction of her life at this point, after almost two-and-a-half years of living on the edge in New York. The music scene was exploding all around her, not only with disco and a burgeoning gay club scene but with the innovations of the synthesizer and of the young Debbie Harry and Blondie, the Talking Heads, the Ramones, The Pretenders, and others who were incorporating rock and roll, disco, pop, punk, and funk into a new amalgam.[19] Add to that the debut of MTV in 1981, which gave music an image and musicians a whole new venue. But Madonna at this point was not even a blip on the screen. According to Gary Burke, she was discouraged enough to even start talking about returning to Michigan.[20]

In March 1981, the band got a break with its first—and then second—gig at Max's Kansas City, a happening downtown club where Warhol held court and Debbie Harry had been a waitress. Making that scene was major exposure for Emmy. Madonna, who already had begun to attract a small downtown cult following, especially in the gay clubs, came out on stage in her usual attention-getting style, this time wearing gray pajamas and sporting red hair in a Chrissie Hynde punk cut. She was hoping that the Gotham Records agent she'd just met on the Music Building elevator and invited to the show was in the audience. But the agent, Camille Barbone, had a migraine and couldn't make it. And Madonna pulled a tantrum about it the next day, right in Barbone's office. It wouldn't be her last.

NOTES

1. Quoted by Andrew Morton. *Madonna*. (New York: St. Martin's Press, 2002). 89.

2. *Truth or Dare*. Directed by Alek Keshishian. Miramax, 1990.

3. Barbara Victor. *Goddess: Inside Madonna*. (New York: Cliff Street Books/ HarperCollins, 2001). 48.

4. *Ibid*.

5. Morton, 88.

6. J. Randy Taraborrelli. *Madonna: An Intimate Biography*. (New York: Berkley Books, Simon & Schuster, 2002). 40.

7. Morton, 96.

8. Taraborrelli, 42.

9. Morton, 91–93.

10. *Ibid.*, 91.

11. Robert Matthew-Walker. *Madonna: The Biography*. (Pan Books/Sidgwick & Jackson Limited, 1991). 33.

12. Victor, 217–221.

13. Morton, 107–108.

14. Matthew-Walker, 44.

15. Morton, 181.

16. *Ibid.*, 110.

17. *Ibid.*, 113.

18. "Discography." www.absolutemadonna.com (accessed 23 September 2006).

19. A good history of the popular music scene in the 1980s and 1990s can be found in Martha Bayles. *Hole in Our Soul: The Loss of Beauty and Meaning in American Popular Music*. (New York: The Free Press, 1994).

20. Morton, 120.

Chapter 3

LUCKY STAR

Madonna knew how to cause a commotion when she wanted something.

On the elevator in the Music Building, she seemed to keep bumping into the same two people, Adam Alter and Camille Barbone. She knew who they were—Alter ran Gotham Records, the only recording studio in the Music Building, and Barbone was a talent agent associated with it. To get their attention, she would come out with some surprising statement—"Do you get it yet?"—or smart remark—"Hey, you look just like John Lennon"—whenever they were on the elevator or in the halls together.[1] Camille was intrigued by this waiflike creature and accepted her invitation to catch the show at Max's Kansas City, but she missed it because she had a migraine. After Madonna's furious outburst in her office about this the next day, Camille made sure she went to see the second show.

Camille, who later said she recognized Madonna as "a nobody who was about to be somebody,"[2] was impressed with her performance at Max's. After listening to Madonna's demo tape, she signed Madonna to a contract with Gotham and became her manager. It was St. Patrick's Day, March 17, 1981, and they celebrated over green beer. Camille Barbone could see Madonna's potential, and perhaps she had visions of giving her own career a boost by turning this unknown into a major star.

She said she felt sorry for Madonna and took her under her wing in a motherly way. Camille offered Madonna $100 a week, a part-time job as a house cleaner, and a place to live off Riverside Drive.[3] But seeing Madonna for her potential as a lead singer, the first thing Camille did was fire her back-up band Emmy, a move that outraged and alienated the band members. She also signed Madonna up for acting lessons, envisioning the possibility of Madonna as a movie star. But Madonna's teacher, Madame Rostova, found her vulgar and unladylike. "I doubt that this girl will ever be taken seriously as an actress," Rostova pronounced, refusing to work with her.[4]

Eventually, the arrangement went way beyond management for Camille. She apparently fell in love with Madonna, who began to exploit the situation even as she thrived under the care of a strong maternal woman. "It isn't true that we were lovers," Camille said later. "But was I in love with her? Yeah! It was a crazy kind of thing, protection, maternal, playing with each other in a very flirtatious way . . . She loves strong women and I was her hero."[5]

They discovered they had the same birthday (although Camille was eight years older), always an important sign for the superstitious Madonna, and for a while they were inseparable, taking vacations together. Camille had given Madonna a safe haven, a place to live and an income. But despite her effort to promote Madonna's career, making a demo tape of four songs that she hawked around to record companies, and booking her into some clubs, Camille was not making any progress with the record deal she had promised. Actually, she was just on the brink of working out a deal for Madonna with Columbia Records when Madonna announced she was ending her relationship with Gotham Records. She walked out, saying that Camille was taking too long to make anything happen and that she didn't like the songs she had to perform anyway.

It was a big blow to Camille, who had staked everything on Madonna and had no other ambition than to make her a star. Madonna said later that Camille was getting too attached to her.[6] All the care and coddling meant nothing to Madonna if her career was stalled. Despite the struggles and hardship she had endured before she met Camille, Madonna was willing to take that life on again if it meant she could move ahead, and she'd already shown she could drop people abruptly when they were no longer of use to her. Later, on her 2006 documentary, *I've Got A Secret to Tell You*, she admitted:

> Let's just say I have less ups and downs in my life. I mean, I'm not going to lie. I had a lot of fun. But I was kind of like a spinning wheel. Life seemed to be a series of random events for me. Sometimes I was ecstatic and happy and sometimes I was depressed. I seemed to be a bit more careless with people back in those days. I don't miss being an idiot. I just feel like I know so much more than I did before, and sometimes I say to myself,

what was I thinking before I was thinking? I won't say I didn't have fun. But sometimes fun is overrated.[7]

THE START OF SOMETHING BIG

It was the spring of 1982. Madonna went back to the Music Building, somehow picking up again with Steve Bray. Living in one of the rehearsal studios, she survived once again by doing part-time jobs, by eating sporadically (a lot of popcorn), and by sheer ambition.[8] Steve and Madonna recorded "Everybody," both words and music by Madonna, along with three other songs including "Burning Up" (also by Madonna), "Ain't No Big Deal," and "Stay," all with the dance beat that was Madonna's music trademark at the time. She began marketing the tape around, trying to get disc jockeys to play it. She persuaded one, Mark Kamins at Danceteria, a hot New York dance club where Sade worked behind the bar and the artist Keith Haring checked coats, to play it. He loved it and so did the club crowd. Sensing her star potential—like so many others—Kamins proposed a partnership that could result in her first album, and Madonna accepted.

Kamins went to see Michael Rosenblatt, an executive at Warner Bros. Records, bringing his protégée along. Rosenblatt wasn't as impressed with the tape as he was with Madonna, who seemed to radiate something special. He offered her a deal, a $5,000 advance plus $1,000 in royalties for each song she wrote. One more signature was required, that of Seymour Stein, the president of Sire Records, the division of Warner Bros. that would manage the contract. The only problem was that he was in the hospital at Lenox Hill recuperating after heart surgery. Madonna asked Rosenblatt to send Stein the tape in the hospital anyway and after hearing it, Stein said he "flipped out"[9] and invited Madonna to come see him at the hospital. He signed her up from his hospital bed. At last, about to turn 24, Madonna had what she had been after for four grueling years in New York City—and she was about to make the most of it.

Indeed, what happened next happened fast. Rosenblatt wanted to release a Madonna single with two of the songs off her demo tape, "Ain't No Big Deal," and "Everybody," but deciding the first song was not going to work, he did an unusual thing and put "Everybody" on both sides of the record. Steve Bray argued that he should be the producer for the single since he had recorded the demo tape, but Kamins, by now into an affair with Madonna, took over. Once again, Madonna and Steve Bray split.[10]

Her single was released in October 1982 and it was a hit, moving quickly up the dance charts. It must have been supremely satisfying to Madonna that her first record and first hit was a song—both music and lyrics—she herself had written. It had a danceable rhythm-and-blues beat that Sire Records had subtly marketed as if Madonna were a black artist, fitting the record into a radio playlist category where it might make headway. In New York, that was on the black station WKTU. People were surprised when they later saw that this "black Madonna" was actually a bleached-blonde white babe.

What turned the tide for Madonna was a three-minute dance act she put on at Danceteria, wearing a top hat and tails and singing "Everybody." In the audience were the Sire Records executives she'd made sure to invite, including Stein and Rosenblatt who, watching her flashy performance, suddenly realized what a visual knockout Madonna was in person. They ordered up an in-house video of Madonna singing "Everybody," which was sent to clubs around the country that were using dance videos.[11] Madonna started to get nationwide attention, propelling "Everybody" to No. 3 on the dance charts and into the *Billboard* Hot 100 list.[12] All of a sudden, Warner Bros., with a small investment, was now actually making some money on Madonna. They began considering her for an album, first trying out a "mini-LP" of "Physical Attraction," a song written for her by Reggie Lucas who would produce the LP, backed with "Burning Up" from the original Bray/Madonna demo tape.

THE FIRST ALBUM

As the LP climbed the charts, Warner Bros./Sire moved ahead with plans for Madonna's debut album. It was originally called *Lucky Star* after a new song Madonna had written for Mark Kamins, but the album came out titled simply *Madonna*, perhaps in recognition that this singular name could have star power. Indeed, Madonna has said:

> My mother is the only other person I have ever heard of named Madonna. I never had any trouble with the name. Not in school or anything. Of course, I went to Catholic schools. And then I got involved in the music industry, everybody thought I took it as a stage name. So I let them think that. . . . It's pretty glamorous.[13]

John "Jellybean" Benitez, Madonna's new boy toy and a DJ at the club Funhouse, offered a song he'd discovered, "Holiday," to Madonna for the album. Written by Curtis Hudson and Lisa Stevens of the group Pure Energy, the song was reworked by Madonna and Jellybean to give it her styling. They got a friend, Fred Zarr, to add the distinctive honky-tonk piano solo. It was a simple song with a fresh appeal and a good mood, an excellent addition to the *Madonna* album, which also included "Borderline," a song written by Reggie Lucas, "Burning Up" (words and music by Madonna), "Physical Attraction," "I Know It," "Think of Me," "Everybody," and "Lucky Star." The album was released in July 1983 and took off. Jellybean's song, "Holiday," boosted the album during the Thanksgiving to Christmas holiday season, and *Madonna* the debut album became a Top 5 hit. She had dedicated it to her father.

In January 1984, riding on the success of "Holiday," Madonna was invited to appear and sing the song on the hit dance show, *American Bandstand*, with Dick Clark. It was her first national television appearance. Clark asked her what she wanted to do when she grew up. Madonna replied, "Rule the world."[14] At least in the world of pop music, that was going to happen sooner than anyone thought.

As biographer Andrew Morton says, the "incredible success" of her debut album "took everyone by surprise—including Warner executives" and made Madonna "a household name."[15] The music was basically rock and roll with a dance beat; Madonna later called it the "aerobics album."[16] Some critics called it New Wave disco. Her voice, with its tight high range and natural lower register, fit well into the very danceable music (although one unkind soul said her voice sounded like "Minnie Mouse on helium"[17]). Nonetheless, what was most distinctive about the album was that Madonna's music jumped traditional niche markets and got play across the board in black, gay, Latino, and disco clubs. Madonna herself also appealed across boundaries. She had the kind of street cred fans could identify with, with her flash-trash style of dress, sassy attitude, and her very visible affairs—both in real life and on video—with black, white, and Hispanic men. Her overt female sexuality helped her become "the personification of a boy's dreams as well as a modern-day role model for liberated girls," according to one biographer.[18]

Her trademark tacky style, complete with belly button and crucifix, was catching on, too, as a fashion statement among club kids and fans. Indeed, the crucifixes she wore as earrings and around her neck became the jewelry of the moment, appearing on fashionable necks all over town. Madonna said she had always carried rosaries around with her and one day just decided it would be "kind of offbeat and interesting" to wear one as a necklace. "I mean, everything I do is sort of tongue-in-cheek," she said: Besides, the crucifixes seemed to go with her name:

> It's a strange blend—a beautiful sort of symbolism, the idea of someone suffering, which is what Jesus Christ on a crucifix stands for, and then not taking it seriously at all. Seeing

it as an icon with no religiousness attached to it. It isn't a
sacrilegious thing for me. I'm not saying, "This is Jesus Christ,"
and I'm laughing. When I went to Catholic schools, I thought
the huge crucifixes nuns wore around their necks with their
habits were really beautiful. I have one like that now. I wear it
sometimes but not onstage. It's too big. It might fly up in the
air and hit me in the face.[19]

Madonna was always going to explain away some of the controversial things she did and the clothes she wore as part of her sense of
humor, as a "tongue-in-cheek" sendup of things she thought people
took too seriously, including sex. Joke or not, Madonna was actually
in the serious process of creating an image for herself, just as other pop
singers at the time like Boy George, with his karma-chameleon outfits and heavy eye makeup, Cyndi Lauper, with her wild orange hair,
and David Bowie, with his constantly changing personae, were already
doing. Prowling the downtown clubs at night with her friends, including Michigan college pals Janice Galloway and Linda Alaniz, now
a photographer, dancer Erica Bell, owner of the Lucky Strike Club,
retailer Maripol, and savvy New Yorker Debi Mazar who sometimes
served as Madonna's makeup artist, Madonna, ever alert to trends,
caught on to the latest in fashion and music before the rest of world
did. As her good friend Debi Mazar said:

Neither of us had any money. We were just young girls trying
to do interesting things in New York City. People weren't
dying yet of AIDS, and here was a small community of artists
and musicians—[Jean-Michel] Basquiat, Keith Haring—and
everybody was together: black, white, Spanish, Chinese. It
was the beginning of rap, and white people and black people
were all together making music. . . . Madonna and I used
to run around and go to the Roxy, go dancing and to art
shows. At the time, we both had a taste for, you know, Latin
boys.[20]

MTV

It helped that Madonna was now getting some exposure on MTV,
which in February 1984 was then in its third year and up to now had
featured mostly male musicians like Van Halen, ZZ Top, and Michael

Jackson. Madonna had made some low-budget videos of "Everybody" and "Burning Up" in 1983, but it was her next video, *Borderline*, that would get the attention on MTV. It was filmed partially in black-and-white to set up the storyline, with Madonna modeling as a glamorous blonde for a professional photographer at his stylish home and then rejecting him for her Latino boyfriend in the Hispanic barrio (filmed in color). By the end of the video, Madonna has petulantly spray-painted the photographer's classical sculptures and fancy car and, crossing borderlines, escapes to the barrio to let her hair down and happily play pool with her boyfriend.

The rush for Madonna fashion took off with her next video, *Lucky Star*, where, against a stark white background, Madonna cavorts in an all-black outfit with leggings, ankle boots, and belly button, her tangled hair tied with a floppy black ribbon. She was actually just wearing what she always wore, an arresting outfit of mesh top and shiny black miniskirt, with one dangling star earring, cut-off gloves, and rubber bangles up her arms. The clothes looked like castoffs plucked from a thrift shop or dumpster, although actually a club-hopping friend, Erica Bell, took credit for designing the outfit.[21] Madonna's teenage fans went nuts for the look and ran out to assemble their own versions of this unconventional garb, guaranteed to upset their parents.

The video was directed by Mary Lambert, a Rhode Island School of Design graduate and filmmaker who would direct some of Madonna's most successful videos, including *Material Girl*. Madonna's riveting performance on this video shows how perfectly she and this new medium meshed, with closeups of her mesmerizing gaze interspersed with visually engaging dance steps. She loves the camera and knows instinctively how to engage it. The song, "Lucky Star," written by Madonna, was released as a single in the summer of 1984 and became the "biggest-selling and fastest-climbing single she had ever had, sending the 'album sales through the roof,' Michael Rosenblatt commented."[22] It reached platinum status when it sold 1 million copies in the United States.[23]

This sudden success meant that Madonna quickly needed some professionals to help manage her career. Jellybean, savvy about such matters, told her about Freddy DeMann, a well-known music manager in Hollywood who had handled Michael Jackson, and Madonna flew out to California to meet him. Whatever wiles Madonna used to convince him to take her on, he did, and the arrangement turned out to be solid gold for both of them. DeMann recalls their first meeting: "She had the most unbelievable physicality I've ever seen in any human. She was enrapturing, she was just captivating, she had the same moxie she has today. She was just unique, wearing her rags and her safety pins."[24]

DeMann's connections and Madonna's ambitions meshed beautifully. He would be her manager for the next 15 years, getting a handsome percentage of her gross earnings. He seemed to understand Madonna and got along with her very well. They were, as Sire Records president Seymour Stein said, "DeMann and DeWoman."[25] It was DeMann who got Madonna her first real movie role in the fall of 1983, a cameo part playing a club singer in Jon Peters's romantic comedy, Vision Quest. As DeMann told Vanity Fair in 1991:

> What you have to understand with Madonna is that she has substance. People forget that. Since she reinvents herself all the time and does these provocative things, people tend to concentrate on her image of the moment. But there is substance there. If you only resort to provocation, you don't last long. Madonna is the biggest star in the universe. And she likes the view.[26]

In another interview in 1992, DeMann said that he and Madonna "seem to fulfill a need in each other. We have a need for approval and accomplishment, and we've accomplished a lot. But we're both hungry. We have to prove ourselves over and over to ourselves and others. Nothing will ever be enough. Never."[27]

Madonna later acquired the publicist Liz Rosenberg who would shepherd her through the snarls and tangles of press coverage for many years, and still does. Rosenberg says she feels like Madonna's Jewish mother. Indeed, she and Freddy DeMann have been like surrogate parents to Madonna, the "grown-ups" in her entourage.

Meanwhile, her relationship with Jellybean blossomed. She had already had a brief three-month affair with Jean-Michel Basquiat, the grafitti artist, whom she met at one of her favorite hangouts, the Lucky Strike Club in SoHo, owned by her friend Erica Bell. A black artist who was being called the James Dean of the art world, Basquiat was beginning to make a name for himself with edgy paintings that seemed to capture the downtown moment. Andy Warhol would take notice and take him under his wing. But Madonna eventually was so turned off by Basquiat's drug habit and constant depression that she broke off the relationship. Sadly, Basquiat died of a heroin overdose five years later at the age of 27, although his paintings live on in museums and wealthy art lovers' collections.

John "Jellybean" Benitz was more on Madonna's wavelength. Ambitious and shrewd himself, he not only helped Madonna further her career but understood her quest for fame. A hot-tempered guy from Spanish Harlem, Jellybean was more than a match for Madonna's own firey moments. Their relationship lasted for almost three years, during Madonna's incredible rise to stardom. They got engaged and moved in together in the SoHo apartment Madonna now could afford and bought with some of her new earnings. Madonna even took him home to Michigan at Thanksgiving to meet her family who were unprepared for the punk outfits they were wearing. "Is that a costume?" her father asked when he saw her.[28]

NUMBER ONE

In September, she had been on the MTV Video Music Awards, popping out of a wedding cake wearing a trashy bridal outfit and singing a new, unreleased song, "Like a Virgin." It would become her biggest hit so far, Number One for six weeks after it came out in November 1984 as part of her second album, also titled *Like a Virgin*. She had been to Venice to film the intriguing and beautiful MTV video of *Like a Virgin* (again directed by Mary Lambert). But then the controversy began, as family organizations complained that the song and video promoted sex without marriage and undermined family values, offering an unsavory Madonna/Whore image. Madonna, who had been using outrage ever since she was little to get attention, was well aware that such controversy was a sure-fire way to get publicity. And her Madonna/Whore image was not going to go away.

The year 1984 was unbelievable for Madonna. Indisputably, she was now the Queen of Pop. It had taken almost six years and Madonna had certainly paid her dues. She was famous; she was getting rich; she had produced two hit albums and had thousands of fans in the United States and beyond. All of sudden, instead of leading an anonymous, transient existence in a hostile city, she couldn't go anywhere without being recognized. Fame wasn't going to be easy for Madonna, but right now, it felt so good.

She had been getting ready for this moment ever since she left Michigan in 1978, never, in all the tough times in New York City, letting go of her vision. She had the survival instincts, even to go without much food and to sleep on studio floors; she had the discipline from her training as a dancer; and, most important, she had the persistence to keep moving ahead despite all the setbacks. What also seems to have kept her going was that deep need for adulation, an assurance, for Madonna, that she was loved. There was still such a feeling of emptiness left by the loss of her mother, as she told *Vanity* Fair magazine in 1992:

I didn't have a mother, like maybe a female role model. I think when you go through something really traumatic in your childhood you choose one of two things—you either overcompensate and pull yourself up and make yourself stand tall, and become a real attention getter, or you become terribly introverted and you have real personality problems.[29]

Madonna said she promised herself "I will never be hurt again, I will be in charge of my life, in charge of my destiny. I will make things work. I will not feel this pain in my heart."[30] She tried, time after time, to fill up the emptiness with the flattering and fawning praise of her fans. Such dogged pursuit of fame, experts say, reflects a deep-seated feeling of abandonment as well as a fear of death. The approval of other people can provide a sense of security and protection, however illusory, and validate one's identity.[31]

Madonna admits to being driven to achieve.

I have an iron will and all of my will has always been to conquer some horrible feeling of inadequacy. . . I'm always struggling with that fear. I push past one spell of it and discover myself as a special human being and then I get to another stage and think I'm mediocre and uninteresting. And I find a way to get myself out of that. Again and again. My drive in life is from this horrible fear of being mediocre. And that's always pushing me, pushing me.[32]

A less driven person might have packed it in and gone back home to the Midwest long ago.

NOTES

1. Andrew Morton. *Madonna*. (New York: St. Martin's Press, 2002). 123.

2. J. Randy Taraborrelli. *Madonna: An Intimate Biography*. (New York: Berkley Books/Simon & Schuster, 2001). 60.

3. Morton, 126–127.

4. Taraborrelli, 62.

5. Morton, 128. See also Taraborrelli, 61; Anderson, 90; Victor, 162.

6. Taraborrelli, 72.

7. *I've Got Secret to Tell You*. Directed by Jonas Akerland. Lucky Lou Productions/Warner Bros., 2005.

8. *Ibid.*

9. Taraborrelli, 75.

10. Morton, 146.

11. Morton, 150–151.

12. *Billboard*, a weekly American magazine, tracks and ranks popular music. The *Billboard* Hot 100 ranks the top 100 songs according to sales. The *Billboard* Hot 200 ranks album sales. Its rankings are considered the standard measure in the U.S. music industry.

13. Quoted by Denise Worrell. "Now: Madonna on Madonna." *Time*, May 27, 1985. www.time.com (accessed August 19, 2006).

14. Morton, 163.

15. *Ibid.*, 159.

16. Taraborrelli, 84.

17. Quoted by John Skow, "Madonna Rocks the Land," *Time*, May 27, 1985. www. time.com (accessed August 19, 2006).

18. Robert Matthew-Walker. *Madonna: The Biography.* (London: Pan Books/Sidgwick & Jackson, 1991). 59.

19. Quoted by Worrell. *Time*. May 27, 1985. www.time.com (accessed August 19, 2006).

20. Quoted by Tarraborrelli, 72–73.

21. Christopher Anderson. *Madonna Unauthorized.* (New York: Island Books/Dell Publishing, 1991). 131.

22. *Ibid.*, 68.

23. In the United States, 500,000 albums sold give an album gold status; 1 million sold is platinum.

24. Maureen Orth. "Madonna in Wonderland." *Vanity Fair* October 1992. 300.

25. Morton, 160.

26. Lynn Hirschberg. "The Misfit." *Vanity Fair*. April 1991. 200.

27. Orth, 301.

28. Anderson, 141.

29. Orth, 306

30. *Ibid.*

31. Benedict Carey. "The Fame Motive." *The New York Times*. 22 August 2006. D1, 6.

32. Quoted by Hirschberg, 198.

Chapter 4

MATERIAL GIRL

For Madonna, fame was a dream come true, but it took some getting used to. She was discovering the cruel paradox of fame, that it robs you of your privacy at the same time it makes you known to all the world. But if fame is indeed a bitch goddess, Madonna was its equal in more ways than one (and not unwilling to be a bitch goddess herself). Now that she finally had the recognition she had long craved, she wasn't going to let it go. "I love being onstage and I love reaching out to people and I love the expressions in people's eyes and just the ecstasy and the thrill," she said at the time.[1] Still, she had to hire a bodyguard. "When I finish a show I can't stop on the street and sign a few autographs because I would be there three years. Sometimes when I go back to my hotel room there are people hiding in the ice closet, waiting. That is scary. I feel caged in hotel rooms wherever I go."[2] Her publicist, Liz Rosenberg, says she told Madonna just "to sit back, reflect, enjoy the success."[3] But that wasn't the way Madonna handled it: "I don't sit around and contemplate my fame or how popular I am. What interests me is what happens in my confrontations with people every day and in my performances at night."[4]

Actually, what interested her most was her family's reaction—or nonreaction—to her fame. Most of all, she wanted her father to recognize her success, but he said nothing. When she went home to Michigan for holidays, it was as if nothing had changed. She still had to sleep in a sleeping bag on the floor, and everybody acted as if she were the same person, despite the obvious signs that she was becoming famous. "At home, nobody brings up the fact that I'm a star," she told *Vanity Fair* magazine. "Not one word. At first I thought, well, how come I'm not getting any special treatment?"[5] Madonna says she doesn't think her father really understood what she was doing when she first moved away. As she told *Time* magazine in 1985:

> He can't imagine that you can make a living from [dancing] or work at it or be proud of it or think of it as an accomplishment. He could never really be supportive about it. It wasn't until my first album came out and my father started hearing my songs on the radio that he stopped asking me questions. I think now he has some conception of my success. He reads about me and people bother him and he has to change his phone number all the time. All of a sudden he's popular, and my brothers and sisters are popular in school because of their association. If he didn't know then, he knows now.[6]

"All my life, I've been going out of my way to get my father's approval. And he's never been impressed," Madonna told *Rolling Stone* in 2005. "I mean, he's only liked certain things I've done: my last tour, *Evita*, *Dick Tracy*, and a couple of my ballads. That's about it."[7] In Madonna's 2006 documentary, *I've Got a Secret to Tell You*, her father concedes that "going into the entertainment business was probably that venue of expression that she needed to fulfill her own needs." Later, after her father saw the completed documentary, he e-mailed Madonna to say for the first time that he approved: "In spite of our differences— I don't agree with everything that you say—I'm very proud of you."[8]

Madonna's MTV videos in 1985 were beautifully directed by Mary Lambert. The *Like a Virgin* video was filmed on location in Venice, with Madonna wearing a wedding dress, writhing in a gondola on the canals, a real lion prowling the precincts and a predator husband wearing a lion mask. The *Material Girl* video was a takeoff on blonde bombshell Marilyn Monroe in *Gentlemen Prefer Blondes* with Madonna in a copy of Monroe's pink strapless dress. The video, with Madonna tossing money (and a bevy of swains tossing her), seemed to endorse materialism—"'Cause the boy with the cold hard cash/Is always Mister Right"—although in the end she drives off with a man in a pickup truck who has presented her with a bouquet of daisies (never mind that he is really a rich guy who just bribed a farmer to lend him the truck). As always, the ambiguities and contradictions of Madonna videos—here, the softer image of Monroe contrasted with the cold-hearted yuppie message—invite viewers to entertain several interpretations at once, Madonna as Hollywood sex goddess, as money-mad materialist, and as girl-next-door.

Certainly, teenage girls bought the images, entranced with Madonna's mix of glamour and rebellion. They had begun to mob her wherever she went, copying her style of dress, the cut-off gloves, the crucifixes, the leggings and ankle boots, the arm full of bangles. No surprise that they became Madonna followers, since she had been aiming at the teenage market anyway with her music. They were dubbed "wannabes" (as in wanna be like Madonna), a fan club of 8- to 14-year-old girls (and older). Macy's even allotted a whole floor section to selling Madonna styles.[9] "Maybe kids now see someone in the public eye doing what I do," Madonna commented. "Maybe that's the phenomenon and why young girls are dressing up like me—because finally someone else is showing that it's O.K."[10] Madonna herself briefly sold a line of her own punk-chic clothing, called Yazoo, at her friend Maripol's Bleecker Street shop that had a whole section marked off as "Madonnaland."[11]

By the start of 1985, Madonna was huge. She was on the cover of *Time* magazine in May and already had four MTV videos out there, including *Crazy for You* from *Vision Quest* and, soon, six singles hitting the charts. In addition, she had landed a part in a low-budget film, *Desperately Seeking Susan*, starring Rosanna Arquette as a bored New Jersey housewife who changes places with club kid Madonna in lower Manhattan and learns about downtown life. Madonna, as Susan, was essentially playing herself, and she was such a hit in the film—which turned out to be the fifth-highest grossing movie of the year—that Arquette, an award-winning actress, complained about being overshadowed. Madonna is indeed irresistible in this movie, a sassy free spirit with the moves and attitude that became her stock in trade. The picture probably offers a good look at the way Madonna actually did spend her first years in downtown New York City, living on the edge, in and out of the clubs, cadging meals and boyfriends, taking baths in public restrooms. The movie's theme song, "Into the Groove" (written by Madonna with Steve Bray), became a huge hit and would be Madonna's next MTV video.

In Los Angeles, in January 1985, to make the *Material Girl* video, Madonna was to meet the man who would become her husband, Sean Penn. Her relationship with Jellybean Benitez was waning, perhaps a casualty of their mutually intense ambitions. Rumors surfaced that she had become pregnant by Jellybean and had had an abortion while she was in California. Their last public appearance together was that January at the American Music Awards in Los Angeles, where Madonna lost out on the Favorite Female Pop Vocalist title to Cyndi Lauper, the pop singer she'd once emulated and saw as a video rival.

LOVE AT FIRST SIGHT

Sean Penn had come to the set of *Material Girl* at the invitation of a family friend, Mary Lambert, Madonna's video director. And Madonna noticed him in his leather jacket and sunglasses, standing off to the side. She later claimed she knew immediately that he was the man she was going to marry.[12] But she was busy dating Prince, whom she had met earlier at the American Music Awards when she had presented him with an award. Prince showed her Los Angeles and invited her to his concert. As the tabloids told it, this was a romantic pairing, but it seemed that Madonna may have been more interested in learning from Prince about how he handled his career than she was in him. The relationship trailed off but, like so many of Madonna's former boyfriends, he remained a friend, even doing a duet with her, "Love Song," on her fourth studio album, *Like a Prayer*.

Sean Penn, the son of Leo Penn, a television director, and Eileen Penn, a former actress, was familiar with Hollywood ways, having grown up in Santa Monica and palled around with other aspiring actors like Rob Lowe, River Phoenix, Matt Dillon, and Tom Cruise. He already had a reputation as a bad boy, which was part of his charm for Madonna. The rigorous acting classes he had taken in Los Angeles had honed him into a disciplined actor. By the time they met, Penn had already appeared twice on Broadway and starred in seven films, including *Fast Times at Ridgemont High* and a Louis Malle movie, *Crackers*, a remake, ironically, of *Big Deal on Madonna Street*.[13] Pauline Kael, the *New Yorker's* movie critic, had compared him with James Dean and Marlon Brando.[14]

Whatever the critics thought, Sean Penn was just Madonna's type. His angry demeanor, his rebellious streak, even his temper, suited her— at least in the beginning—and matched her own transgressive style. There was allure, too, in his Hollywood milieu and Penn's own passion for his career. Although she never mentioned it publicly, Sean faintly resembled her father, with his slightly downturned mouth and facial expression, and despite his reputation, Sean had some of her father's old-fashioned values. In addition, Madonna was happy to discover that she and Sean had practically the same birthday in August, a day apart (Madonna found such coincidences very significant), although he was two years younger. They were both Leos, an astrological sign said to favor big egos.

Theirs was an exciting courtship, conducted on both coasts and sandwiched into their own demanding career schedules. Madonna was on the cover of *Time* magazine in May (headlined, "Why She's Hot") and she was about to begin her first concert tour, *The Virgin Tour*, to open in Seattle in April 1985. Sean was getting ready to spend two months filming another movie, *At Close Range*, with his brother, Christopher Penn, and Christopher Walken in Nashville, Tennessee. He managed to be on hand in Seattle for the opening of Madonna's tour however, and was there again later in Detroit, where Madonna performed on tour for her own father and family (a "squeaky-clean" show, one fan said).

In June, during a brief sojourn in Nashville (and bouncing naked on their hotel room bed),[15] Sean asked Madonna to marry him and she accepted. There had already been rumors that Madonna was pregnant by Sean and had had an abortion. If true, it would have been her second abortion in less than a year.

They decided to get married on her 27th birthday, August 16, 1985, just three months after getting engaged. Realizing that the wedding could be a potential paparazzi nightmare—they had already been chased many times through the streets of New York by photographers and reporters—they decided to hold the ceremony at a beautiful house hidden high on a cliff near Malibu, owned by a friend of Penn's family, real estate developer Dan Unger.

Meanwhile, as Madonna and Sean were happily planning their wedding, those nude photographs she had posed for in her hungry days six years ago resurfaced, having fallen into the hands of Bob Guccione at *Penthouse* and Hugh Hefner at *Playboy*. Published in the July 10 issue of *Playboy* and later in *Penthouse*, the pictures soon appeared in the media all over the world. Hugh Hefner had even sent a copy of the magazine directly to Sean, who was reportedly unfazed by it all. Madonna was angry and unnerved. Still, ever the trooper, she managed to perform three days later, as agreed, at Bob Geldolf's *Live Aid* concert in Philadelphia before 90,000 people and an international television audience.[16] Madonna, whose appeal to the gay community had been apparent from her very earliest performances in downtown clubs, was one of first performers to get involved in AIDS relief, having suffered the loss of several close friends to the disease, including her dance instructor and mentor Christopher Flynn and artists Keith Haring and Martin Burgoyne. She has raised substantial sums of money for the cause.

MR. AND MRS. SEAN PENN

Madonna had already made one wedding gown famous in her video, *Like a Virgin*, but she wanted her real gown to be special, something that

Grace Kelly might have worn, as she told the designer, Marlene Stewart.[17] The result was a white strapless dress in taffeta and chiffon, which Madonna wore with a veil and, her special touch, a black bowler hat. Her maid of honor was her younger sister, Paula. She hired the famous Los Angeles restaurant, Spago, where Wolfgang Puck was chef, to cater the wedding, and sent out 220 invitations to a guest list that included such Hollywood and media luminaries as Cher, Andy Warhol, Keith Haring, Steve Rubell, Carrie Fisher, Christopher Walken, Martin Sheen, Tom Cruise, and Diane Keaton.[18]

Madonna and Sean had gone to great lengths to make sure the media did not know when and where the wedding would be, even omitting the time and place on the invitations (they called the guests just 24 hours ahead of time to tell them). Somehow, however, the reporters and photographers found out and the couple's open air ceremony by the swimming pool was loudly punctuated by press helicopters and surrounded by paparazzi in the bushes. Sean had already carved out a giant message to the press down on the beach—"Fuck Off"—and even fired warning shots with a pistol at the helicopters, but the reporters were not to be deterred. The wedding (and Madonna's 27th birthday) turned into a circus despite their best efforts, and the guests could barely hear the couple say their vows before Judge John Merrick.

Nonetheless, they got to spend a quiet wedding night at Sean's parents' house and later, after celebrating Sean's 25th birthday the next day, left for the Highlands Inn in Carmel, California for their honeymoon, cut short by the arrival again of the hassling press and the public. For their first home together, they considered moving to New York City and applied for a co-op apartment at the exclusive San Remo on the Upper West Side, but were turned down by the co-op board, apparently for fear the couple would attract paparazzi and because of the nude photographs.[19] (Later, Madonna purchased another New York apartment on Central Park West.) The newlyweds ended up buying a big Spanish-style house in Malibu where they installed extensive security and hired "minders" to protect Madonna. Sean even had spikes put on top of the iron fence surrounding the Malibu property.[20]

PAPA DON'T PREACH

Madonna was already into her next project that fall, writing songs and recording for her third studio album, *True Blue*, titled as Sean's favorite phrase. She brought back Steve Bray and hired a new song-writer collaborator, Patrick Leonard, to help, although she herself co-wrote all but one of the nine tracks. "La Isla Bonita," written by Pat Leonard originally for Michael Jackson who turned it down, was a departure in sound and ambience for Madonna. With a lilting Latin beat, the song evokes the tropics; the video started a craze for the ruffled skirts and blouses Madonna wore in it.[21] Another song, "Papa Don't Preach," written by Brian Elliott with additional lyrics by Madonna, went to Number One on the charts soon after its release and stirred up the kind of controversy Madonna certainly must have anticipated. Telling the story of a teenager who is afraid to tell her father she is pregnant and wants to keep the baby, the song and the later video were condemned by feminists and both sides of the abortion issue for seeming to condone teenage pregnancy and as an antiabortion message (prolife organizations actually applauded that). Magazine headlines asked, "Should Papa Preach?" and "Does Madonna's Hit Encourage Teenage Pregnancy?"[22] Even though Madonna was almost 28 years old when she made the video, she managed to pull off a teenage look in a black leather jacket, jeans, and a gamin cut. The actor Danny Aiello played her father. Directed by James Foley, a Hollywood friend who had been best man at the wedding, the video told the story convincingly, with short takes of a more sophisticated-looking Madonna singing and dancing in a black bustier, her hair now a bleached blonde.

Foley directed the video for another song on the album, "Open Your Heart," staged as a peepshow with sleazy male patrons peering through windows to watch Madonna (again blonde in black bustier)[23] writhing on a chair. After the show, Madonna leaves the theater hand-in-hand with a little boy as they dance into the sunset. It was this ending that stirred up criticism and controversy once again, family groups objecting that the video suggested child abuse. Madonna, used to pushing people's buttons, did not flinch.

Madonna's videos actually break the rules of music videos, one critic says. Her videos use a "multilayered structure of images" that, instead of merely illustrating the lyrics as most videos do, generate "sometimes complex meanings proliferating in the play of the music, lyrics, and images." These images are often densely packed and can be processed on different levels by different audiences, from teenagers indulging their fantasies to "more sophisticated music and cultural critics."[24] Moreover, Madonna can *act* in a three-minute video in a way she was not able to do so well in a full-length film. Picking high-calibre talent to direct her videos has been a smart move as well.

WEDDED WOE

All along, Sean and Madonna had had some very public tiffs during their engagement, and these didn't stop once they were married. They were two very independent-minded people with tempers and egos, and perhaps the standoffs were inevitable. The press had a nickname for them, the "Poison Penns." Sean did not want to be known as "Mr. Madonna," and apparently he was not prepared for what marriage to America's emerging pop star queen would bring. "At twenty-four I didn't realize the difference between a great first-time date and a lifetime commitment," he observed.[25] On the other hand, Madonna said she enjoyed the domesticity of marriage. "I did the wash a lot. I liked folding Sean's underwear. I liked mating socks. You know what I love? I love taking the lint out of the lint screen," an admission that seems totally at odds with her public persona.[26]

Domesticity was all well and good, but the constant press harassment and lack of privacy whenever they were out in public got to Sean, and he responded to intrusions by slugging a few photographers and, unfortunately, a songwriter friend of Madonna's, David Wolinski, who pressed charges.[27] Sean was fined and given a year's probation,[28] which, after several more fistfights and a bout of heavy drinking, turned into a 60-day jail sentence a year later in the summer of 1987. He served 30 days of it in Mono County, California, and was allowed out for a film performance. He was released in September.[29]

While he was in jail that summer, Madonna, meanwhile, was on her second concert tour, Who's That Girl?, which would take her to Europe and Japan for the first time as well as throughout the United States. The tour was named to promote the film she had made in the fall of 1986, playing a streetwise character named Nikki Finn and co-starring with Griffin Dunne. The film, Who's That Girl?, opened to much fanfare at Radio City in August of 1987, but the box office was disappointing and once again, Madonna's ongoing quest for a film career failed to launch.

She and Sean had already acted together in another box-office clunker, Shanghai Surprise, co-produced by George Harrison of the Beatles and filmed in Hong Kong. Madonna played a missionary, with Sean as a gangster she falls in love with. The filming did not go well and when it was released in August 1986, critics found Madonna's performance wooden and accused her of being able only to play herself. Harrison had invested some $17 million to make the film, but it grossed only $2.2 million and quickly faded away.[30] In the last week of August that summer, Madonna made her first appearance on stage, enjoying the chance to act with Sean in a short, experimental run of a David Rabe play, *Goose and Tom-Tom*, at New York's Lincoln Center for a selected audience of celebrities who were polite about her performance; no critics were invited. Sean managed to slug two photographers outside a restaurant on opening night.[31]

Madonna's international *Who's That Girl?* tour, however, already performed to sell-out crowds in the United States, was a huge success. It opened in Japan and finished in Italy, where some of her Ciccone relatives from Pacentro, the village where her grandparents were married, came to visit her after the concert in Turin. She gave them a warm welcome, although some of them were outspoken about their American relative's reputation for outrageous behavior and style of dress.[32] Some Pacentro residents proposed putting up a 13-foot statue of a bustier-wearing Madonna in the town square and making her an honorary citizen, but the proposal was vetoed by the mayor, who feared that a statue of Madonna as a role model might corrupt the morals of Italian young people.

Returning home at the end of the summer, exhausted from the tour, Madonna was greeted by Sean, out of prison but drinking and disappearing for days at a time. In November, he resurfaced at their New York apartment, expecting to have Thanksgiving dinner with Madonna. Instead, Madonna went out to Brooklyn by herself to have dinner with her little sister, Melanie.[33] Sean went back to Los Angeles and went on a binge. Early in December of 1987, Madonna filed for divorce.

NOTES

1. Quoted by Denise Worrell. "Now: Madonna on Madonna." *Time*, May 27, 1985. www.time.com (accessed August 19, 2006).

2. *Ibid.*

3. Quoted by Maureen Orth. "Madonna in Wonderland." *Vanity Fair*, October 1992: 301.

4. Quoted by Worrell. *Time*, May 27, 1985.

5. Quoted by Lynn Hirschberg. "Madonna in Wonderland." *Vanity Fair*, April 1991. 198.

6. Quoted by Worrell. *Time*, May 27, 1985.

7. Neil Strauss. "How Madonna Got Her Groove Back." *Rolling Stone*, December 1, 2005. 76

8. *Ibid.*

9. Andrew Morton. *Madonna.* (New York: St. Martin's Press, 2001). 166.

10. Quoted by Worrell. *Time*, May 27, 1985.

11. Robert Matthew-Walker. *Madonna: The Biography.* (London: Sidgwick & Jackson Limited, 1991). 93.

12. Morton, 172.

13. Robert Matthew-Walker. *Madonna: The Biography*. (London: Pan Books/ Sidgwick & Jackson Limited, 1991). 98–99.

14. *Ibid.*, 98.

15. Morton, 179.

16. Matthew-Walker, 103.

17. Morton, 182.

18. Matthew-Walker, 105.

19. Barbara Victor. *Goddess: Inside Madonna*. (New York: Cliff Street Books/ HarperCollins, 2001). 277.

20. J. Randy Taraborrelli. *Madonna: An Intimate Biography*. (New York: Berkley Books/Simon & Schuster, 2002). 121.

21. Morton, 199.

22. Taraborrelli, 123.

23. The black bustier Madonna wore in the *Open Your Heart* video was later stolen from the Frederick's of Hollywood lingerie museum.

24. Douglas Kellner. "Madonna, Fashion and Identity." In *On Fashion*, edited by Shari Benstock and Susanne Ferriss. (New Brunswick: Rutgers University Press, 1994). 173.

25. Quoted by Morton, 206.

26. Quoted by Lynn Hirshberg, "The Misfit." *Vanity Fair*, April 1991. 196.

27. Morton, 193.

28. *Ibid.*

29. *Ibid.*, 198.

30. Taraborrelli, 123.

31. Christopher Andersen. *Madonna Unauthorized*. (New York: Island Books/Dell Publishing, 1992). 225.

32. Victor, 71.

33. Andersen, 266.

Chapter 5

TRUTH OR DARE

Less than two weeks later, Madonna had changed her mind about divorcing Sean. She withdrew the divorce papers in January 1988. They were to stay together just one more year, however. Although it seemed that she genuinely loved Sean, the tension of living with a husband so volatile and so at odds with her over their mutual career ambitions had made their private life unpredictable and constantly upsetting. Sean was moody and hard to live with. Madonna was hardly an easy companion either, and during most of their last year as a married couple, they were frequently apart, often on opposite coasts. Early in the year Sean was in Asia filming again, starring in *Casualties of War* with Michael J. Fox.[1] Madonna, in New York and not ready to give up on her own film career, had just finished filming *Bloodhounds of Broadway*, a movie based on the stories of Damon Runyon and starring Matt Dillon, Jennifer Grey, and Randy Quaid. Madonna played the part of Hortense, a singer and dancer in a 1920s speakeasy. The film wasn't released until 1989 and despite its stellar cast and artistic aspirations, it opened to negative reviews. Madonna was also considered for a part in Francis Ford Coppola's third *Godfather* film, but the director ended up casting his own daughter, Sofia, in the role.

MADONNA ON BROADWAY

Madonna was still looking for a way to establish herself as an actress, a quest that so far had yielded little evidence of acting talent. Critics continued to find her film performances wooden and unconvincing, perhaps because she seemed to choose roles that demanded more in range and ability than she could offer. Still, that spring, Madonna went for a big one, auditioning for a part in a Broadway play, David Mamet's *Speed-the-Plow*.[2] She got the part, beating out 30 other aspirants. She would play the role of Karen, a seemingly mousy secretary, in a story about two successful movie executives (played by Joe Mantegna and Ron Silver) who bet they can bed their new secretary. Madonna/Karen shows her spirit by seducing one of them instead and squelching their next big project. Needless to say, having Madonna in the play made it a sellout. It became known as the "Madonna play" even as critics—once again—agreed that she still needed acting lessons. The verdict in a headline from the *New York Daily News:* "NO, SHE CAN'T ACT."[3] Madonna wasn't happy with her performance either, but blamed the playwright for changing the character she thought she was playing. She had seen Karen as an innocent; Mamet wanted her played as a ruthless schemer. Madonna was upset when she realized this, sometimes leaving the rehearsals in tears.[4]

Jacqueline Kennedy Onassis, along with other celebrities, was in the audience on opening night May 3, 1988, not so much to see the play apparently but to check out Madonna who had started seeing her son, John F. Kennedy, Jr. He and Madonna had met at a party in December[5] and had been secretly going out together that spring. Madonna was quite taken with him and he with her, to all reports,[6] but Jackie was apparently not at all happy that her son was involved with Madonna, perhaps remembering her own husband's involvement with another celebrity, Marilyn Monroe. The relationship came to an end that summer, possibly because Jackie did not approve.

Meanwhile, Madonna had begun hanging out with another new friend, Sandra Bernhard, the comedian, whom she had met earlier in Los Angeles. Alike in many ways, they shared a sassy attitude and enjoyed keeping people guessing about their relationship. Whether or not there was any truth to it, they pretended to be lesbians. Madonna, asked later about her possible sexual relationships with women, said she preferred "hetero sex." "I have a lot of sexual fantasies about women, and I enjoy being with women, but by and large I'm mostly fulfilled by being with a man." Implying that she has tried sex with women, Madonna said, "It's not the same."[7] She and Bernhard enjoyed scandalizing people, most famously on the David Letterman show and at the New York clubs they frequented. Most scandalized of all was Sean Penn, who, when he got back home to Malibu from filming in Asia, was outraged to find that Sandra Bernhard had moved in on his marriage. Madonna was using her friendship with Bernhard as a good way to get under Sean's skin, even taking her as her "date" to the opening night in Los Angeles of Sean's new play, *Hurly Burly* by David Rabe. Needless to say, Sean was outraged yet again.[8]

BREAKING UP IS HARD TO DO

The marriage was rocky enough without all this deliberate provocation. Sean's temper and his drinking continued to escalate. In December that year, Madonna asked him to move out and, surprisingly, he did, going back to live at his parents' house in Santa Monica. But a few days after Christmas, Sean came back to their Malibu house, climbed a fence, broke into the house, and tied up and tortured Madonna for nine hours. Somehow she escaped, lip bleeding and makeup smeared, and drove to the police station. Although he told a different version of the story, Sean was arrested. Madonna decided not to press charges.[9]

Instead, she filed for divorce in early January 1989, citing, in the language of the law, "irreconcilable differences." By the end of the month, with the previous divorce filing still fresh on the books, they were divorced. Sean said he did not want any of the $70 million Madonna had earned while they were married and took only his own movie earnings, about $5 million. He kept the Malibu house; she kept the New York apartment.[10]

Madonna moved to a $3 million, seven-bedroom house once owned by Rudolph Valentino that she bought in the Hollywood Hills, near the big white Hollywood sign. She asked her brother, Christopher Ciccone, who had become a designer, to decorate it, using the paintings Madonna had already begun to collect. (Her publicist, Liz Rosenberg, once said that what Madonna wants to do when she grows up is "to be Peggy Guggenheim," the famous and flamboyant art collector.)[11] Madonna was especially taken with the work of Frida Kahlo, whose vivid paintings appealed to her for their emotion and color. Perhaps Madonna could also relate to Frida who had been married to a violent man, the painter Diego Rivera (Madonna also angled for a part in the later movie about Frida Kahlo but lost out to Salma Hayek). Madonna, like Barbra Streisand, collected the work of Tamara de Lempicka and hung one of her large paintings in her bedroom. She also has works by Picasso, Ferdinand Leger, and Salvador Dali.

Madonna's three-and-a-half year marriage to Sean was now over, and she has always spoken of this with regret. Could she have done something about his drinking? Doubtful. She was 30 years old and had achieved the highest pinnacles of American pop stardom, but the loss of the man she once called "the coolest guy in the universe" was a major emotional downer." As she told *Vanity Fair* magazine in 1991:

> It's a big loss. But let's face it—Sean and I had problems. We had this high-visibility life, and that had a lot to do with the demise of the marriage. When you're always being watched, you almost want to kill each other . . . Sean was very protective of me. He was like my father in a way. He patrolled what I wore. He'd say, "You're not wearing that dress. You can see everything in that." But at least he was paying attention to me. At least he had the balls. And I liked his public demonstrations of protecting me. In retrospect, I understand why he dealt with the press the way he did, but you have to realize it's a losing battle. It's not going to get you anywhere. And I don't think Sean can give that up. He'll defend you to the death—it's irrational, but also noble.[12]

Although they both were to remarry (he married Robin Wright in 1996), for Madonna there would always be a tinge of sadness about the man she had regarded as a soul mate.

THE POPE BANS MADONNA

In the months after the divorce, however, there were plenty of projects to help Madonna get her mind off Sean. Her fourth studio album, *Like a Prayer*, dedicated to her mother ("who taught me how to pray"), was released in March 1989; and the soft drink giant, Pepsi, made a $5 million deal to feature her and the title song (written by Madonna and Patrick Leonard) in a major two-minute commercial to be shown worldwide. The *Like a Prayer* video—which showed Madonna (clad in a dark maroon slip dress) singing and writhing in the nave of a church and kissing the feet of a black saint—was, however, stirring up all kinds of controversy. Part of the controversy was the racial component of the video in which Madonna, dancing in front of burning Ku Klux Klan crosses, rescues an innocent black man who has been accused of stabbing a white woman. The imagery and lyrics suggested that there was a sexual component, as Madonna, lying in a pew, dreams of lovemaking with the black saint: "In the midnight hour, I can feel your power/Just like a prayer, you know I'll take you there." Stigmata appear on her hands.

The mix of the sacred and profane in the video upset the Vatican. The Pope banned any appearances of Madonna in Italy. Madonna had tapped into the eroticism underlying some religious rituals and made them explicit. Director Mary Lambert commented, "I felt it was a song about ecstasy and very specifically sexual ecstasy and how it relates to religious ecstasy."[13] Certainly, Madonna's own Catholic upbringing was an influence.

> Whether you end up believing it later or not, Catholicism gives you a strength, an inner strength. I think maybe the essence of Catholicism I haven't rejected, but the theory of it, I have, if that makes any sense. . . . The thing that has remained with me most, I guess, is the idea that you do unto others as they do unto you.[14]

Her message in the video was, essentially, about racial equality. But the public didn't take it that way. The American Family Association denounced it and even an Islamic organization protested it as blasphemous (Jesus is regarded as a prophet in Islamic faith). Realizing that religious groups were going to boycott them, Pepsi yanked the commercial off the air. Nonetheless, they let Madonna keep the $5 million advance, staving off what would surely have been a lawsuit.[15]

Needless to say, "Like a Prayer" became the Number One single on the *Billboard* charts. The album sold in the millions both in the United States and abroad, and the video itself won Viewers Choice at the MTV Music Awards in 1989. *Rolling Stone* said the album was proof that Madonna should be taken seriously as an artist. Whatever the Vatican and other religious groups thought of her, the American public loved Madonna. At the MTV Awards, she brazenly thanked Pepsi "for causing so much controversy."[16]

Another song on the album, "Express Yourself," was the basis for a video that was also controversial, featuring a crotch-grabbing Madonna imitating Michael Jackson's famous gesture. She was dressed in an androgynous Marlene Dietrich black suit with slits to show off the corset underneath and wearing a monocle. The video's images are based on the 1930s Fritz Lang modernist film, *Metropolis,* which explored class issues. Madonna appropriates its futuristic and industrial images for an exploration of male and female relations. The most controversial scene showed her wearing a collar chained to a bed, then lapping up milk from a saucer like a cat. Feminists had a fit, but Madonna replied that she was not oppressed in these scenes because she *chose* to enact them. She did complain, though, about the criticisms of her crotch-grabbing, saying that if male singers like Michael Jackson can get away with it, why can't a woman?

WARREN BEATTY AND *DICK TRACY*

One of the Hollywood stars Sean had introduced Madonna to early in their marriage was Warren Beatty, who got in touch with Madonna in the fall of 1988 about a role in his new film, *Dick Tracy*. While Beatty was said to prefer Kathleen Turner or Kim Basinger to play the role of Breathless Mahoney in the movie, he was impressed with Madonna and she got the part. She also got the man. Beatty, one of Hollywood's established stars, became another of her conquests. By the time filming started in February 1989, they were a Hollywood couple, despite the difference in their ages (he was 22 years older than she). Madonna also recorded the soundtrack album, *I'm Breathless (Music from and Inspired by the Film Dick Tracy)*, a bonus for Disney, the distributor of the film, and for Warner Bros.

STRIKE A POSE

One of the new songs Madonna added to the album was "Vogue" (written with Shep Pettibone), which capitalized on a current dance trend in the gay clubs of posing as a model or celebrity. The song, with its "Vogue" rap of names—"Greta Garbo and Monroe, Dietrich and DiMaggio, Marlon Brando, Jimmy Dean, on the cover of a magazine"—went straight to Number One on the charts. The black-and-white *Vogue* video, directed by David Fincher, was ultra-stylish, one shot of Madonna showing her striking a pose in a corset in homage to a famous Horst photograph. Both the song and the video were huge hits, not only in the gay community, which loved her anyway, but worldwide. The song, "Vogue," became her "all-time, best-selling" single to that point.[17] For the 1990 MTV Music Awards, Madonna and her dancers performed the song on stage in period eighteenth-century costumes with Marie Antoinette wigs, she flipping her hoop skirt provocatively.

Blond Ambition

The movie *Dick Tracy* came out in June 1990. This time, the critics raved about Madonna's performance. At last she could enjoy her first onscreen success since *Desperately Seeking Susan*; 1990 was definitely her year. She had been the top American pop star for a straight five years and she was embarking on her next international tour, *Blond Ambition*,[18] which would take her to Japan, Canada, Britain, Italy, and Spain, as well as the United States, where she got to sing "Happy Birthday" to her father who had made the trip to Chicago to see her show. Madonna managed to cause a commotion on the tour, particularly in Toronto, where police threatened to shut down her performance for public indecency. They objected to the "Like a Virgin" scene where she writhed on a velvet bed simulating masturbation while two of her dancers, wearing large conical breasts (designed by Jean-Paul Gaultier) strapped to their chests, fondled her. Madonna went ahead with the performance and toughed out the threat. She has always regarded her performances as art and she made the argument she always did in such situations, that, as an artist, she was entitled to free expression. Amazingly, the Toronto officials backed down, claiming that her performance had gone off without incident and that they found nothing indecent about it.[19] Perhaps Madonna's refusal to back down and the claim that her manager, Freddy DeMann, made that it would be "a worldwide scandal" if the Toronto officials shut down the show could have changed their minds.

Truth or Dare

In addition to sellout crowds and controversy, the tour would be memorialized in a documentary, *Truth or Dare* (known as *In Bed with Madonna* in Europe). Madonna herself had authorized the documentary and picked a relatively unknown filmmaker, 25-year-old Alek Keshishian, to direct it. He was a Harvard graduate who had sent her his pop opera incorporating some of her music. Apparently she was impressed. Although the film, done in black and white (with color segments for the concert scenes), was intended mainly as a behind-the-scenes look at Madonna on tour, it functions as a kind of biography, with footage of her father and stepmother, as well as her brothers and sisters and one of her girlhood friends. Warren Beatty is in it, too, commenting at one point, "She doesn't want to *live* off-camera, much less talk." Madonna herself comments at another point in the film that Sean Penn was the love of her life, a remark that she tried to have edited out, unsuccessfully. Keshishian captures many such off-guard moments, filming the backstage action using a hand-held camera that gives the effect of a home movie.

Madonna is shown holding a prayer circle with her dancers and back-up singers before every performance. She calls herself "Mama," and says her entourage made her start "feeling like a mother to them. I picked a lot of emotional cripples. And it fulfills a need in me to be mothered." With a cough drop in her mouth, Madonna prays that they all will give their best performance ever and go out there and "kick ass." She asks her father after the show if it was too "racy" for him; he replies, diplomatically, that "a couple of scenes could be left out." Madonna's encounter in the film with her girlhood friend, Moira McPharlin, is brisk and rather heartless. Moira has presented Madonna with one of her own paintings and asks Madonna to be godmother to her unborn baby. Without committing herself, Madonna brings up some embarrassing moments in Moira's past and leaves. Moira turns to the camera and says, "That little shit."

In another scene, Madonna sticks her finger down her throat and pretends to gag after Kevin Costner tells her he thought her show was "neat." Even though there are many scenes of Madonna hugging her dancers and cavorting with them, she comes off in the documentary as very controlling and ego-driven. In many scenes backstage, she is shown being made up and barking orders from the makeup chair. Madonna *is* demanding, but given her own perfectionism and discipline, she expects a lot from her entourage. Several of her dancers later sued her over the film, claiming invasion of privacy, fraud, and deceit. Eventually, however, they settled out of court.[20]

There are telling scenes with Madonna and her brothers in the documentary. Martin, the second oldest, just out of alcohol rehab, is supposed to stop by after her show but arrives too late to see Madonna. He's shown knocking on the door where she is sleeping, then leaving, disappointedly. Later in the film, he says that having such a famous sister makes him feel that he should have done more with his life. "How come you're not this, how come you're not that?" he asks himself. Madonna seems closest to her youngest brother, Christopher, who designed all the sets for the tour, although she outs him as gay in the film. (She had already done it in an interview with *Advocate* magazine earlier, much to his dismay.) She keeps up with her sister Melanie and her husband, Joe Henry, but her relationship with her other sister, Paula, seems to have always been clouded by Paula's jealousy of Madonna. Paula, equally attractive and a good singer, always seems to have felt that she should be the star.[21]

Warren Beatty hovers in the background in several scenes, at one point calling the chaos surrounding Madonna "insane." She calls him "pussyman." Beatty, who had already lived through the publicity frenzy of being a star with such acclaimed and influential films as *Bonnie and Clyde* and *Shampoo* in the 1960s and 1970s, was bored with public relations hoopla. But he still had a taste for young women and undoubtedly enjoyed being connected to Madonna's celebrity. Now that *Dick Tracy* had been released and Madonna's tour was finished, however, their relationship seemed to be on the wane. Beatty had given Madonna a six-carat diamond and sapphire ring at one point, seemingly as a promise of engagement, but he later told her it was just a friendship ring.[22] He began to distance himself from her, eventually ending the relationship. Magazines and news coverage reported the break up as a blow to Madonna's pride. She was not used to being the one rejected, and she considered Beatty, a man who had pampered her and shown her what life among the Hollywood elite could be like, her conquest. The most hurtful part, perhaps, was that just a year after the breakup, Warren Beatty married Annette Bening.

In less than two years, Madonna had lost out with two of the most important men in her life, Sean Penn and Warren Beatty. She was at the peak of her career so far, rich beyond her wildest dreams, and famous all over the world. She was not a product of some music industry idea; Madonna had created her own image and won her own place in pop music (and she resented suggestions that she had slept her way to the top). But all that public adulation, something she had worked so hard for, must have felt a little hollow compared to the dearth of love in her private life. It may even have been a root cause of her problems with these men. Sean and Warren were accustomed to fame in their own right, but not to living in the shadow of someone else's fame or, least of all, being "Mr. Madonna." Even her serious relationship with Jellybean Benitz had foundered on issues like this. If Madonna was going to find happiness with a man, she would have to find someone who wasn't competing with all the celebrity frenzy surrounding her.

NOTES

1. Andrew Morton. *Madonna*. (New York: St. Martin's Press, 2001). 209.

2. The title, *Speed-the-Plow*, refers to an old English farming term meaning good luck and a profitable season of plowing.

3. Quoted by Morton, 204.

4. Morton, 202–204.

5. *Ibid.*, 207.

6. Christopher Andersen. *Madonna Unauthorized*. (New York: Island Books/Dell Publishing, 1991). 267–268.

7. Quoted by Maureen Orth. "Madonna in Wonderland." *Vanity Fair*, April 1991. 306.

8. Morton, 211.

9. Barbara Victor. *Goddess: Inside Madonna*. (New York: Cliff Street Books/HarperCollins, 2001). 310.

10. J. Randy Taraborrelli. *Madonna: An Intimate Biography*. (New York: Berkley Books/Simon & Schuster, 2001). 171.

11. Quoted by Orth, 301.

12. Quoted by Lynn Hirschberg. "The Misfit." *Vanity Fair*, April 1991. 196.

13. Taraborrelli, 180.

14. Quoted by Denise Worrell. "Now: Madonna on Madonna." *Time*, May 27, 1985. www.time.com (accessed August 19, 2006).

15. Morton, 218.

16. Taraborrelli, 181.

17. Morton, 219.

18. Madonna has not explained why she chose the masculine spelling of "blond" instead of the feminine "blonde" for the title of this tour.

19. *Truth or Dare*, directed by Alex Keshishian, Miramax, 1990.

20. Taraborrelli, 237.

21. Victor, 129; Morton, 57.

22. Taraborrelli, 201.

Chapter 6

BORDERLINE

Not that Madonna would ever be at a loss for a boyfriend. She already had her eye on a much younger man, Tony Ward, a 26-year-old who had been an extra in two of her videos, *Like a Prayer* and *Cherish*. She spotted him again on the beach at Malibu, and by September 1990, tall, dark, and handsome Tony Ward had moved into Madonna's house in the Hollywood Hills. They became an item in the celebrity gossip columns, cavorting around Hollywood. By December, Madonna was pregnant. Her doctors warned that there were life-threatening complications with the pregnancy and recommended that she terminate it. Reluctantly and sorrowfully, she did.[1]

It was just as well, because Tony had a secret he hadn't yet told Madonna: he was a married man. Right before Christmas, the truth came out; he had gotten married just after they met on the Malibu beach, but couldn't resist the chance to fulfill a dream of being with Madonna. She must have known he wasn't husband material for her anyway; he had become her "boy toy" of the moment, on the rebound from Warren Beatty. She gave him his walking papers after a big, vase-smashing fight at a Christmas party. He moved out and Madonna moved on.[2]

PUSHING THE ENVELOPE

The next phase of her career, from 1990 through 1996, was indeed going to take her moving in a whole new direction. Emotionally battered by her experiences with men, perhaps more cynical but, as always, very shrewd, Madonna began to push the envelope of outrage to keep herself in the public eye, exploring the boundaries of taste and sexuality. But first, at the end of 1990, she produced a greatest hits album, titled, ironically, *The Immaculate Collection*, a kind of musical voyage through her career so far. It included Madonna's first singles, "Holiday, "Lucky Star," and "Borderline," as well as 13 more of her hits, 8 of which had been at the top of the charts. As a retrospective of her climb to success, it solidified Madonna's story and her status as America's pop icon. And it included at least one song guaranteed to upset people.

"Justify My Love," the song, and the video directed by the avant-garde French director Jean-Baptiste Mondino explored the world of lesbianism and transsexuals, with Madonna herself engaged in fondling and kissing them and Tony Ward acting out some of the footage with her. Filmed in black and white at a Paris luxury hotel, the Royal Monceau, the video included nudity and erotic scenes and fantasies. MTV had planned to debut the *Justify My Love* video during its "All Madonna Weekend" beginning December 1, 1990, but suddenly announced before airing it that MTV program executives were banning the video as "religiously and sexually offensive."[3] There was some press skepticism about whether or not this was preplanned or genuine, but having the video banned couldn't have worked better for Madonna, who stirred the pot by protesting loudly about the unfairness of it all. The *Justify My Love* video sold 400,000 copies that Christmas.

Madonna showed up at the Academy Awards show on March 25, 1991, on the arm of Michael Jackson, an unlikely but sensational pairing that got both of them plenty of attention. Wearing a low-cut Bob Mackie gown and $20 million worth of jewels on loan from Harry Winston, Madonna was an attention-getter all by herself, let alone having Michael Jackson as her date. She stole the show at the Awards that night, singing "Sooner or Later" from the soundtrack of *Dick Tracy*, and to her delight, the song won the Academy Award for Best Song. It was quite an evening and got them both plenty of press, which was, essentially, the point.

In May, she was in Cannes for the 44th annual International Film Festival, presenting her documentary, *Truth or Dare*, to the world and to positive reviews. Sean Penn was there, too, with *The Indian Runner*, a film he had written and directed. Perhaps Madonna wanted to make sure he knew she was around. It was hard to miss her as she stepped out of her limo wearing a dazzling red cape she threw open to show off a cone-shaped bra and see-through girdle,[4] causing a commotion as usual among the throngs waiting to catch a glimpse of her.

Meanwhile, Penny Marshall had offered her a part in a new film, *A League of Their Own*, to star with Rosie O'Donnell, Geena Davis, and

Tom Hanks in a story about a women's baseball team in the 1940s. Filming began in July in Evansville, Indiana; Madonna, typically, prepared for the role of Mae Mordabato by learning everything she could about baseball, even visiting some of the country's top ball players. She played her part well, essentially a toned-down version of herself, and critics gave her good reviews as a comedienne. The film earned big grosses when it was released in the summer of 1992. In addition, Madonna and Rosie O'Donnell became good friends.

THE *SEX* BOOK

Madonna had also been at work putting together her infamous *Sex* book, another strategic move to upset the public and generate media attention. She hired top drawer talent to help her produce the book. It was photographed in black and white by well-known photographer Steven Meisel who took 20,000 frames, with art direction by *Harper's Bazaar* art director Fabien Baron and editing by writer Glenn O'Brien. The book featured Madonna in various stages of undress and sexuality, depicting what she said were her own sexual fantasies: kissing women (including Isabella Rossellini, Ingrid Casares, and Naomi Campbell), cavorting with Tony Ward (again) as well as with another former boyfriend, Vanilla Ice, and with rapper Big Daddy Kane. She posed suggestively with a dog, hitchhiked in the nude on a Miami highway, and ate pizza in nothing but a pair of high heels. *Vanity Fair* called it "the dirtiest coffee-table book ever published."[5] Madonna, on the other hand, claimed it was all in fun and couldn't understand why people didn't get the sense of humor in it. "I don't have the same hang-ups that other people do, and that's the point I'm trying to make with this book," she told Maureen Orth in an interview published in *Vanity Fair* magazine when the *Sex* book came out.

> I don't think that sex is bad. I don't think that nudity is bad. I don't think that being in touch with your sexuality and being able to talk about it and being able to talk about this person and their sexuality [is bad]. I think the problem is that everybody's so uptight about it that they make it into something bad when it isn't, and if people could talk about it freely, we would have more people practicing more safe sex, we wouldn't have people sexually abusing each other because they wouldn't be so uptight to say what they really want, what they really feel.[6]

But how does that square with photographs of Madonna pumping gas at a Miami service station wearing nothing but black lace leggings, or her frolic with skinheads, complete with nipple piercings and whips, or the one of her bound and gagged threesome with two women? "It's meant to be funny, not scary," Madonna said.[7]

The book was beyond erotic, it was pornographic. Published in October 1992 by Time Warner, the book, tightly sealed in mylar, had covers made of stainless steel with just one word, "Sex," cut into them. The text, written by Madonna, who assumes the identity of 1930s French film star Dita Parlo, describes her views in handwritten letters on sex, love, and the innumerable ways of enjoying one's sex life, sometimes in quite graphic detail and with emphasis on sadomasochism: "You let someone hurt you who you know would never hurt you. It's always a mutual choice. . . . I don't even think S and M is about sex. I think it's about power."[8] As she says in her *Sex* book, "There's something comforting about being tied up. Like when you were a baby your mother strapped you in the car seat. She wanted you to be safe. It was an act of love." On another page, she comments, "I wouldn't want a penis. It would be like having a third leg. It would seem like a contraption that would get in the way. I think I have a dick in my brain."

Madonna explains her philosophy of porn in one of the less graphic pages of *Sex*:

> I don't see how a guy looking at a naked girl in a magazine is degrading to women. Everyone has their sexuality. It's how you treat people in everyday life that counts, not what turns you on in your fantasy. If all a person ever did was get off on porno movies I would say they are probably dysfunctional sexually, but I don't think it's unhealthy to be interested in that or get off on that. I'm not interested in porno movies because everybody is ugly and faking it and it's just silly. They make me laugh, they don't turn me on.

Controversy over the *Sex* book was inevitable. Feminists and religious groups condemned it and Madonna herself for making money from such degrading material. Nonetheless, *Sex*, priced at $49.95, flew off the shelves as fans stormed the bookstores clamoring for a copy. The book climbed to Number One on *The New York Times* bestseller list and sold 1.5 million copies worldwide (the book is out of print, although undoubtedly there are copies for sale on eBay). Reviewers called the book childish and the sex boring,[9] but Madonna got what she wanted, plenty of attention. Yet as one biographer suggests, the *Sex* book, as much as it did attract widespread attention and publicity, was perhaps Madonna's way of putting up a barrier between herself and the public.[10] There is an antisocial aspect to all that sexual provocation and outrage, as if she were mooning the public for trying to intrude on her private life. As *Vanity Fair* commented at the time, "Surely, *Sex* is a middle finger raised to those who preach 'family values.'"[11]

Madonna wasn't done yet with her campaign of outrage either. Her next album, *Erotica*, released at the same time as the *Sex* book in October 1992, was required to carry a warning: "Parental Advisory: Explicit Lyrics." MTV showed the *Erotica* video only after midnight and only three times. The picture on the album cover of Madonna bound and gagged was straight out of the *Sex* book. Directed by Fabien Baron, the *Erotica* video features Madonna playing a dominatrix in a variety of S&M outfits and acts. The album did not sell well, and fans were beginning to wonder if Madonna had finally gone too far on this sex and sadomasochism kick. Even her father called up and asked her to "stop being so racy."[12] Indeed, while her venture into explicit sexual images and lyrics generated plenty of publicity, much of it negative, it was reaching a tipping point. Madonna was trashing her image. One columnist, Molly Ivins, called her a "reigning sex goddess [who] is someone you wouldn't take home if she were the last woman left in the bar."[13]

Ignoring all the negative press, Madonna next chose to star in a movie that did nothing to salvage her reputation. She played yet another bad girl in *Body of Evidence*, Rebecca Carlson, who is accused of murdering a rich man by having repeated sex with him (reportedly, some moviegoers cheered at the end when her character was murdered).[14] The movie also starred Joe Mantegna and Willem Dafoe, actors Madonna admired. Some said that in this movie, Madonna was trying to emulate Sharon Stone, who had played a nymphomaniac the year before in *Basic Instinct*. None of the luster of Stone or the other well-known actors came off on *Body of Evidence*, however, and when it was released in January 1993, the critics savaged the movie. It tanked at the box office and Madonna won another "Razzi" Golden Raspberry Award for Worst Actress. A second movie released that year, *Dangerous Game*, with Madonna playing another nymphomaniac, went straight to video.[15]

MAVERICK

The movies and the *Sex* book had the distinction, however, of being produced by Madonna's own company, Maverick (the name was devised from the first letters of Madonna and Veronica, and last letters of Frederick [DeMann]), formed in April 1992 with Time-Warner to release albums, films, and books (in 2004, Madonna, in a dispute with Warner Bros., sold her shares in the Maverick record label). She had already set up several other companies, including Boy Toy for her music and record royalties; Siren Films, replacing Slutco, for film and video production; Webo Girl for music publishing; and Music Tours, Inc. for live performance contracts.[16] If nothing else, Madonna, as always, needed to be in complete control of her work, and she spent a great deal of time keeping track of her businesses, delegating little of the task to others. *Forbes* and *Fortune* magazines wrote feature articles about her business acumen, applauding her for being so financially savvy. Few of her fans were aware of this side of Madonna. Like Mae West before her and to whom she was often compared for other reasons, Madonna kept her eye on her money even as she played the blonde sexpot. *Forbes* said Madonna had "a brain for sin and a bod for business" and called her "America's Smartest Businesswoman" in its September 1990 cover story about her and other high-earning entertainers.[17] About her success, Madonna says:

> There is a lot of business stuff. But that didn't come as a surprise. Besides, I love meetings with suits. I *live* for meetings with suits. I love them because I know they had a really boring week and I walk in there with my orange velvet leggings and drop popcorn down my cleavage and then fish it out and eat it. I like that. I know I'm entertaining them and I know that they know. Obviously, the best meetings are with suits that are intelligent, because then things are operating on a whole other level.[18]

Unfortunately, Madonna had not been so savvy about the direction of her career at this point. She was clearly on the wrong track and getting a lot of hate mail by now. According to her brother Christopher, bad reviews and negative public reaction actually do bother her, more than she lets on. "People who don't think the controversies and the press affect her are wrong," he says. "She doesn't work up a strategy for all this attention. It's just who she is and what she does. And there is definitely a cost."[19]

It *was* starting to sink in that she needed to soften or change her image. Typically, in answer, she went on tour again in the fall of 1993, this time with a toned-down *Girlie Show*. It was more like a circus than another S&M exhibition, with Madonna playing a burlesque queen, a tamer version of her racy persona as a dominatrix. Limited to 20 venues in the

United States and overseas, the tour was a sellout success. Still, Madonna managed to enrage patrons in Puerto Rico when she rubbed the Puerto Rican flag between her legs. Her show in Israel had to be canceled when Orthodox Jews protested its sexual nature.[20]

She couldn't resist playing the provocateur either when she was on *The Late Show with David Letterman* in March 1994, famously using the f-word 13 times and trying to unsettle Letterman, waving her panties at him and telling him to smell them. Of course this behavior made the headlines in the tabloids, and Madonna would later say she regretted it. A *New York Post* critic called the performance "a pathetic reach for celebrity and notoriety by a woman short on talent and wit" with nothing to sell but shock.[21]

Adding insult to injury, columnist Earl Blackwell, who produced attention-getting lists of the Best and Worst Dressed women every year, named Madonna one of the worst-dressed women of 1994, coming in at Number 10 on his 35th annual list. "Let's be blunt," he said, "yesterday's Evita is today's Velveeta." He'd listed her once or twice before, but she'd shrugged it off, mainly because she had already set off such a fashion craze among the young for her trashy style of dressing. "I used to be a brazen, outgoing, crazy lass," Madonna told Ingrid Sischy in her first *Interview* magazine cover story in 1985. "I went out of my way to make statements with my clothing. . . . I would wear one orange sock and one purple one. . . . I loved seeing the visual effect I had on people."[22] It's no surprise that she said one of her role models was the chameleon singer and performer, David Bowie.

TOUR COUTURE

As she grew more famous, Madonna became a lot more interested in high fashion and had the money to indulge in it. She also had a direct connection to Paris couture through French designer Jean-Paul Gaultier, who had dressed her for her last two concert tours. His avant-garde style of unusual designs, including the cone bra bustier she would wear for her next tour, *Blond Ambition*, suited her outré taste perfectly. She even agreed to model in his spring/summer fashion show in Paris that fall, sashaying down the runway and causing a mild sensation. Karl Lagerfeld of Chanel said he admired Madonna as a trend-setter and called her "the single greatest fashion influence in the world"; Andre Leon Talley of *Vogue* magazine said he thought she was "a goddess of fashion."[23] It helps that Madonna caught the expert eye of stylist Arianne Phillips in 1997. She has been Madonna's fashion advisor ever since. Madonna says of Phillips, who won an Oscar in 2006 for costume design in *Walk the Line*, "She is like me in that she likes to mix high and low when it comes to fashion and she is as inspired by books and art and music as she is by Halston, Balenciaga and Gaultier."[24]

Madonna also had a taste for Gianni Versace's clothes and was good friends with his sister, Donatella. In March 1995, she posed in a series of ads for Versace. Even though what she wore in public was often only one color, black, her outfits had designer labels, and as she got older—and richer—her taste became more refined and her clothes more expensive, mostly from Italian designers like Versace, Prada, and Gucci. She also loves shoes and owns hundreds of pairs, most of which stay in the closet where she visits and admires them.[25] A year after Earl Blackwell's worst-dressed listing, in the fall of 1995, Madonna was presented with the Most Fashionable Artist award at VH1's Fashion and Music Awards. The surprise presenter was her ex-husband, Sean Penn.

The big question about any woman pushing 40 these days seems to be, "Has she had work done?" a reference to plastic surgery. The only "work" Madonna has owned up to is a collagen treatment from a Beverly Hills plastic surgeon to make her lips look plumper (the problem is that the treatments have to be repeated every four months to maintain the look and perhaps Madonna got tired of it).[26] She has an oxygen facial machine in each of her houses and gives herself regular oxygen facials, which her publicist, Liz Rosenberg, says are "phenomenal" for pumping up energy levels and combating jet lag.[27] In addition to rigorous daily runs, Madonna also works out on a Personal Power-Plate vibrating platform, designed to prevent cellulite and osteoporosis.[28]

Needless to say, Madonna has managed to maintain her figure at the 36(C)-24–34 proportions and 115 pounds she's nearly always weighed (she once thought about insuring her breasts but changed her mind). With her dancer's discipline and a rigorous exercise program of running, weight lifting, and workouts she began in earnest in the mid-1980s, her figure changed from soft and curvy to a buns-of-steel, athletic look.

> My whole life is in a constant state of disarray, and the one thing that doesn't change is the workout. . . . If I had nothing to do, I would stay in the gym forever. It's a great place to work out aggression, or, if you're feeling depressed about something, you get on the Lifecycle and you forget it. If you've failed in every way in your day, you've accomplished one thing—you've gotten through your workout and you're not a total piece of shit.[29]

Now she says she gets depressed if she doesn't work out every day; at one time she was running up to 10 miles every morning. "I'm hardest on myself," she admits. In her own words:

> If I have a 7 o'clock call for Woody's movie, I'll get up at 4:30 to exercise. If I don't, I'll never forgive myself. A lot of people say it's really sick and an obsession. Warren used to say I exercised to avoid depression. And he thought I should just go ahead and stop exercising and allow myself to be depressed. And I'd say, "*Warren*, I'll just be depressed about not exercising!"[30]

As her fans know, her hair color is another story. It's been every shade from black and her natural brunette to platinum blonde and red. She claims, "I don't go overboard really in any direction. I don't shave the side of my head. My hair is not pink."[31]

TONING IT DOWN

Madonna's fifth studio album, *Bedtime Stories*, released in 1995 by her own company, Maverick, seemed designed to placate all the criticism she'd endured for the past few years. It offered a new sound, closer to R&B and hip hop than to the characteristic Madonna dance track, with songs about unrequited love and ballads like "Take a Bow," which made it to Number One on the *Billboard* charts. Such luminaries as Sting, Herbie Hancock, Bjork (who wrote "Bedtime Story" for the album), and Kenny "Babyface" Edmonds were listed in the credits. The album cover pictured a softer-looking blonde Madonna in a white dress. Another album released later that year, *Something to Remember*, was a reprisal of Madonna hits including "Crazy for You," "Take a Bow," and "Oh Father," as well as several new songs.

Although the albums were well received, it was clear that Madonna's career needed a major infusion to stay in the music mainstream, and it wasn't going to come from the shock tactics of the past five years. She was going to be 37 in 1995. Her private life was in shambles. She had been running through boyfriends since the Beatty breakup, and her biological clock was starting to tick loudly. Madonna wanted a child, and she had no suitable father in sight. It didn't help that Sean Penn and his wife, Robin Wright, had started a family or that Warren and Annette would soon do so. During the photography shoots for *Sex*, many of which took place in Miami, she became deeply involved with her personal bodyguard, Jim Albright, who was 11 years younger. The relationship continued into 1994 and led her to talk about having a family with him.

STALKER

During the *Sex* photography shoot, Madonna fell in love with Florida and bought the house on Biscayne Bay where they were shooting, having talked the owners, the Nordstrom family, into the sale with an offer near $5 million.[32] She would end up escaping to this new home when a stalker began showing up on her Los Angeles property in the spring of 1995 and threatening her. He was Robert Hoskins, a 27-year-old drifter, who had been sending her letters signed, "Your husband, Bob."[33] Celebrities, by nature of their very public exposure, tend to attract stalkers, and Madonna was no different; perhaps she was even more vulnerable because of the provocative nature of her image. As her publicist, Liz Rosenberg, said when the *Sex* book came out, "Psychos might see there's a message in it for them."[34]

Looking out her Hollywood Hills window one morning, Madonna saw Hoskins on the grounds and alerted her security people who grabbed him and called police. Madonna was frightened enough to leave town. She fled to her house in Miami, only to learn that Hoskins had come back again to the Hollywood Hills house and accosted a guard, who shot him three times. Hoskins recovered, and the case came to trial eventually in Los Angeles in February 1996. Madonna, who was subpoenaed as a witness, could not even look at Hoskins in the courtroom. He was convicted of stalking and sent to jail for 10 years, but Madonna said she continued to have nightmares about the whole affair.[35]

Although Albright stood by her throughout the rough times after the publication of *Sex*, Madonna was beginning to be restless again and started seeing other people, including, improbably, Dennis Rodman, the quirky 6' 7" New York Knicks basketball player. Madonna is only 5' 4½" tall and they made a bizarre-looking couple. Their well-publicized two-month affair did nothing to help her image, and Rodman himself did the relationship in by writing about their sex life in his autobiography and talking to *Playboy* about her performance in bed.[36]

Albright was also trying to bow out of the picture by this time, tired of Madonna's infidelities and a relationship that was so difficult to maintain. In addition, Madonna had lately taken up with a woman friend, Ingrid Casares, whom she had met on South Beach in Miami and featured in her *Sex* book. Casares, the daughter of a Cuban-exile millionaire and later a nightclub owner, was constantly seen with Madonna, giving rise to rumors that there was a lesbian relationship going on, rumors similar to those that Madonna and Sandra Bernhard had provoked. Whatever the truth, Casares seemed to be Madonna's new best friend and she was definitely getting in the way of Albright's relationship with Madonna. By January 1994, he and Madonna had split.

CARLOS LEON

Madonna had found a replacement by the middle of the year. He was Carlos Leon, a 28-year-old Cuban fitness trainer who lived in the South Bronx and whom Madonna had met once at a party. This time, she spotted him running in Central Park and asked a member of her entourage to arrange a meeting. Madonna was quite taken with this quiet, almost shy man, and they began what was to be a long relationship. Leon was different from the "bad boy" types Madonna usually chose and seemingly, he could handle the celebrity frenzy she inspired. By her 37th birthday the next year, Madonna was once again telling friends that she and her boyfriend were going to start a family together.

Meanwhile, Madonna had had her eye on doing another film for some months when news came at Christmas of 1994 that the British director Alan Parker (*Fame, Bugsy Malone*) had been chosen to film *Evita*, the story of Eva Peron, the wife of Argentinian leader Juan Peron, with Andrew Lloyd Webber and Sir Tim Rice. Madonna sat down and put together a handwritten, four-page letter to Parker, telling him why she was the right person for the part of Eva Peron. It was a letter that would change the direction of her languishing career.

NOTES

1. Christopher Andersen. *Madonna Unauthorized*. (New York: Island Books/Dell Publishing, 1991). 352.

2. J. Randy Taraborrelli. *Madonna: An Intimate Biography*. (New York: Berkley Books/Simon & Schuster, 2002). 216–217.

3. *Ibid.*, 222.

4. Andersen, 368.

5. Maureen Orth, "Madonna in Wonderland," *Vanity Fair*, October 1992. 206.

6. *Ibid.*, 212.

7. *Ibid.*

8. *Ibid.*

9. Taraborrelli, 243.

10. *Ibid.*, 242.

11. Orth, 298.

12. Quoted in Taraborrelli, 251.

13. Quoted in Taraborrelli, 246.

14. *Ibid.*, 249.

15. *Ibid.*, 250.

16. *Ibid.*, 234.

17. *Forbes*, September 1990, quoted in Anderson, 343.

18. Quoted by Lynn Hirschberg. "The Misfit." *Vanity Fair*, April 1991. 200.

19. *Ibid.*, 196, 198.

20. Andrew Morton. *Madonna.* (New York: St. Martin's Press, 2001). 267.

21. Taraborrelli, 253–254.

22. Quoted by Ingrid Sischy in "Letter from the Editor," *Interview*, March 2001.

23. Anderson, 344.

24. Ruth La Ferla. "Stepping Out of Hollywood's Dressing Room." *The New York Times*, March 5, 2006. Sunday Styles, 12.

25. Taraborrelli, 346.

26. Andersen, 341.

27. Quoted on "Page Six," *The New York Post*, February 18, 2006.

28. Mary Tannen. "Lovelier Bones." *The New York Times Sunday Magazine*, February 26, 2006. 144.

29. Quoted by Hirschberg, 198.

30. *Ibid.*

31. Quoted by Denise Worrell. "Now: Madonna on Madonna." *The New York Times.* May 27, 1985. www.time.com (accessed August 19, 2006).

32. Morton, 238.

33. Taraborrelli, 259.

34. Quoted by Orth, 298.

35. Taraborrelli, 273–275.

36. Morton, 270.

Madonna at age five in 1963 (the year her mother died). Christopher Andersen Collection.

Madonna in 1966, First Holy Communion. Globe Photos.

Madonna, wearing her Boy Toy belt, sang "Like a Virgin" at the 1984 MTV Music Awards. Getty Images.

Madonna's date for the 63rd Academy Awards Show was Michael Jackson. She stole the show in diamonds and furs, singing "Sooner or Later" from the movie Dick Tracy, which won an Oscar for Best Song. Getty Images.

Madonna, Guy Ritchie, and Rocco John Ritchie (in bunny suit) leave Dornoch Cathedral in Scotland after Rocco's christening, December 21, 2000. Reuters Pictures.

Madonna and her daughter Lourdes, emerging from their limousine in London, January 29, 2002. Reuters Pictures.

Madonna's latest look, a Farrah Fawcett hairdo, March 2006. Photofest.

Chapter 7

REINVENTION

Madonna's letter to director Alan Parker about his new movie, *Evita*, was, naturally, all about why she would be perfect for the part of Eva Peron, the Argentinean First Lady who had captured the hearts of her countrymen as the wife of dictator Juan Peron. In the letter, Madonna argued that "only I could understand her passion and her pain," commenting later that it seemed "as if some other force drove my hand across the page" as she wrote.[1]

Parker was actually considering other actresses for the role, including the leading contender Michelle Pfeiffer, as well as Glenn Close and Meryl Streep. Andrew Lloyd Webber, who with Sir Tim Rice had written the 1978 Broadway musical of *Evita*, was against casting Madonna in the role, but Rice seemed to think she would be right for it. He put in a good word with Webber. And, as it turned out, because Michelle Pfeiffer was pregnant with her second child and might have difficulty with the film schedule, Madonna did eventually get the part. Being cast in *Evita* was a once-in-a-lifetime chance for her, not only in pursuing the success in film that had always seemed to elude her but in reinventing herself and her career at a time when she was slipping out of the spotlight.

Madonna was well aware of the stakes. In characteristic fashion, she threw herself into learning everything she could about Eva Peron and Argentine history. She took tango lessons and signed up with a vocal coach to improve the quality of her singing (all the dialogue in the movie, like the Broadway show, was entirely in song). She flew to Buenos Aires to do more research, where she was greeted with graffiti saying "Evita lives, get out Madonna."[2] Protesters burned an effigy of her, outraged that a performer with her reputation would play the part of their still-beloved Evita (despite the fact that Eva Peron had her own unsavory past). Madonna decided to keep a diary about her experiences: "I knew I was in for the ride of my life. I wanted to remember every detail," she wrote. "By the time this movie comes out, I will have been living vicariously through her for two years."[3]

Madonna wanted to *be* Evita, even visiting her grave. She wore brown contact lenses to match Eva Peron's eye color, covered the gap in her front teeth with a bridge, and wore the same kinds of classic 1940s New Look suits Peron preferred. The downy stray hairs along her hairline were clipped to give her the look of Eva Peron's broader forehead[4] and Argentineans were amazed at how much Madonna came to resemble her. Madonna claimed that she had been fascinated by Eva Peron all her life. Indeed, there were many similarities in their lives. Both came from big families in small towns and escaped to the big city (Eva Peron to Buenos Aires, Madonna to New York City) to find fame and fortune, and both struggled with many setbacks before achieving success. Generations apart, both women aspired to acting careers and traded on their looks and image to get ahead. And both became among the most powerful and successful women of their time.

Perhaps what fascinated Madonna most was Eva Peron's drive and ambition, so similar to her own. Eva Duarte had also lost a parent, her father, at an early age. Born in Argentina in 1919, Eva and her mother and sisters had to go to work as cooks to survive after the death of her father when she was seven. At 15, she left home to go to Buenos Aires, with little money and knowing no one. After some years of struggle, Eva became a radio host and actress (and eventually ended up co-owning the radio station). She dyed her natural brunette hair to blonde when she was cast in a 1938 movie, *Marie Antoinette,* and remained a blonde ever after, wearing her hair in complicated styles.

In 1944, she met Colonel Juan Peron and married him in 1945 (after the marriage, all Eva's movies were banned in Argentina). Peron was so popular with the *los descamisados,* "the shirtless ones"—the workers and poor of Argentina—that the Argentine president feared a coup and had him arrested. When Peron was released from prison, he campaigned for the presidency himself, assisted by Eva, who was becoming known as Evita, the friendly Spanish diminutive for "little Eva," on the campaign trail. She used her weekly radio show to campaign for her husband, talking about her rise from humble beginnings in order to align herself with the workers. Peron was elected president, and Evita took on a prominent and popular role by his side.

She began to wear Paris couture and beautiful jewelry, saying that this was uplifting to the masses and expected of the First Lady. On a European tour the next year, she met with the Pope and heads of state in Spain and Italy and handed out 100 peseta notes to poor children. Returning home, she plunged into charity work, establishing the Eva Peron Foundation for the poor and homeless and working to get the vote for women with the Female Peronist Party. Her efforts helped get Peron elected to a second term as president and vaulted Evita herself to saintly status among the Argentinean working class (the upper classes had always disliked her for her humble roots and lack of education). By now, she had streamlined her look to appear more serious, wearing only business suits and putting her blonde hair in a severe bun. In famous speeches from the balcony of the Casa Rosada, the official government house, she galvanized crowds with her rhetoric and was called the "Spiritual Leader of the Nation."

Celebrating her husband's reelection in the inauguration parade, Eva had to be propped up under her fur coat with a wire frame because she could not stand. Although she did not let on until the end a year later, she had become seriously ill with uterine cancer. She died at age 33, and the entire nation went into mourning, shutting down all activities. Evita remains to this day a hallowed icon in Argentina.[5]

Hers was a story ripe for the telling and, recognizing it, Andrew Lloyd Webber put it on stage in his Broadway musical of *Evita* in 1978, the year Madonna arrived in New York. There is no record of Madonna's seeing the show, but the importance of being blonde and linked to a man of power could not have been lost on her. While Webber and his collaborator, Tim Rice, streamlined Evita's life story and set the entire dialogue to music, the basic theme of Evita as a power blonde success story remained and attracted Madonna in 1994 when the movie was being proposed and cast. Yet, as much as she felt she fit the role, Madonna repeatedly tried to change things in the script to suit herself and to show Evita in a more favorable light. This effort was stonewalled by the director, Alan Parker.

At one point in the filming, Madonna requested an interview with Argentina's President Carlos Menem to discuss using the Casa Rosada as a setting for the movie. When Menem finally agreed to see her, Madonna took a helicopter to meet him at a lavish estate outside Buenos Aires. She thought he was a very seductive man; he told her she looked just like Evita and kept eyeing her straying bra strap.[6] During dinner, Madonna asked if he would change his mind and allow her to film on the balcony of the Casa Rosada, where Eva Peron had stood to address her followers. He said, "Anything is possible," and finally, two weeks later, sent word that he had agreed to allow this. Madonna said that as she was singing "Don't Cry for Me Argentina" on that balcony, she felt Evita enter her body "like a heat missile," pushing her to feel things.[7]

BABY, BABY

The movie was filmed in Hungary, as well as Buenos Aires, with the soundtrack recorded in London. During all the travel and filming, Madonna continued to keep her diary, recording her thoughts and feelings about the project. Published in *Vanity Fair* just before the movie was released at Christmas 1996, the diary also reveals her discovery, as filming progressed, that she was 11 weeks pregnant. The father, not surprisingly, was Carlos Leon. Things were happening a little ahead of schedule. Madonna had hoped that she and Leon would start a family together, but not until the filming of *Evita* was finished. Now Madonna found herself suffering from morning sickness on the set and worrying about how her pregnancy would affect the film schedule.

> Being pregnant should be cheering me up, but it's not. I keep having this nagging feeling that I'm going to destroy what we've all worked so hard to accomplish. I feel like a 14-year-old who is trying to hide the fact that she is pregnant from her parents. It makes me feel like I have something to be ashamed of. The people who do know congratulate me when they find out, but this embarrasses me. Why? Haven't figured this out yet. I feel like we are all in a race against time. How will I do all those glamorous photo shoots to promote the film when I can't even fit into my costumes? What will the press do when they find out?"[8]

She wanted to keep the pregnancy a secret as long as she could, but as usual, the press soon found out and *The New York Post* put the news on the front page in April. She called Carlos and she called her father, hoping he'd be happy. Some people suggested that Madonna had gotten pregnant for shock value and that she was using the father as a stud service. Her reply: "These are comments only a man would make. It's much too difficult to be pregnant and bring a child into this world to do it for whimsical or provocative reasons."[9]

As criticism mounted about Madonna's becoming a single mother and thus not a good role model for young women, she complained to her diary that there were plenty of others like Susan Sarandon,

Goldie Hawn, and Mia Farrow who had children and weren't married to the father:

> What a hypocritical society we live in! I believe people would be more comfortable if I got married and the marriage failed. . . . Women who are educated, women who call themselves feminists, women who are gay have the nerve to attack me in the press and say that my choice to have a baby and not be married is contributing to the destruction of the nuclear family. . . . They are afraid I will raise my baby (à la Joan Crawford in *Mommie Dearest*) all alone in a dark mansion.[10]

As it happened, both the film and the baby were greeted with good press. The baby, named Lourdes Maria Ciccone Leon, was born by cesarean section on October 14, 1996 in Los Angeles, weighing 6 pounds 9 ounces. The name "Lourdes" is, not coincidentally, also the name of a sacred shrine in France to the Virgin Mary, a place Madonna's mother had always longed to go. Lourdes, who goes by the nickname Lola, is 10 years old now, a pretty curly haired brunette who looks like her mother and has Leon's coloring. The relationship between Madonna and Lourdes's father Carlos, however, gradually came to an end. He gave Madonna sole custody of their daughter, but he continues to be a strong presence in Lola's life.

Evita, released on Christmas Day in 1996, was highly praised, as was Madonna's performance in it as a singer, dancer, and actress. The soundtrack album from the movie, including "Don't Cry for Me Argentina" and "You Must Love Me," reached Number Two on the *Billboard* 200 album chart. Madonna eventually won a Golden Globe Award for her acting in *Evita*, with critics complimenting her on her successful re-creation of Eva Peron and on her musical performance. Now 38 years old, Madonna had at last triumphed on screen and achieved her dream of having a child, both in the same year. She had reached another turning point in her career, reinventing herself and her image with the public.

MELLOWING OUT WITH MOTHERHOOD

From all reports, Madonna plunged into motherhood with the same fervor she gave to her career. She loved it, calling the birth of her daughter a "rebirth" for herself. She had put her Hollywood Hills house on the market (for $6.5 million)[11] before the baby was born and bought a cozier, Mediterranean-style house in the Los Feliz section of Los Angeles. Madonna turned her workout room into a nursery for

Lourdes and devoted herself to taking care of her new baby daughter, breastfeeding her, getting down on the floor to play games with her, having fun dressing her up, and taking her on excursions. Madonna seemed to mellow out with motherhood, confessing to be surprised at what it felt like to love something so much and be loved so much in return.

Still, she was not about to give up on a career that had righted itself after *Evita* and the birth of Lourdes. Although she took a year off to care for her new daughter, by March 1998, Madonna was releasing her first new studio album in four years, *Ray of Light*. It won her her first Grammy award in 1999 as Best Pop Album, as well as three more Grammys for Best Dance Recording, Best Short Form Music Video, and Best Record Packaging. Called one of her finest, the album reveals Madonna's voice as a more mature, expressive instrument, putting emotion into electronica, as one critic said. The album included songs about her daughter's birth, her joy and her losses, with "Drowned World," "Frozen," and "Beautiful Stranger," the song she had recorded for Mike Myers's new film, *Austin Powers: The Spy Who Shagged Me*, and which went on to win a Grammy in 2000 as Best Song Written for a Motion Picture.

Madonna and her manager of 15 years, Freddy DeMann, parted company in 1996, for unexplained reasons. Apparently DeMann's protégé, Guy Oseary, and Madonna had wanted him to leave; they bought out DeMann's shares in Maverick in 1999. Her new manager was Caresse Henry of Q-Prime, who stayed with Madonna until 2004 when, in another parting of ways, Caresse was replaced by Oseary and his partner Angela Becker. DeMann now manages pop star Shakira; Caresse has signed on to manage Jessica Simpson.

Madonna had become involved with a new boyfriend just before filming *Evita*. His name was Andy Bird, a British actor and screenwriter whom she had met in Los Angeles through Alek Keshishian, the director of her documentary, *Truth or Dare*. Andy Bird was tall and good-looking and 10 years younger than Madonna. He took her to meet his parents in England at Stratford-on-Avon, and they rented a house in Chelsea while Madonna, who had been thinking of moving to London with her daughter, looked at real estate. Andy came back with her on her business trip to Los Angeles and wound up moving in. The relationship had its ups and downs, duly reported by the tabloids. Once, reportedly, Madonna kicked him out and he went back to London where he took a job as the doorman at the posh Metropolitan Hotel. Eventually Madonna decided she'd had enough of him. There had been a moment when she thought he might be the one to father another child. About to turn 40, Madonna wanted to give Lourdes a brother or sister. In fact, she did become pregnant with Bird's child and worried about whether an abortion would jeopardize her chances of having another child. But two months into the pregnancy, she ended it.[12]

In 1998, Madonna signed to star in yet another movie, *The Next Best Thing*, with Rupert Everett, about a woman who accidentally becomes pregnant by a gay friend. Once again, as she had done with *Evita*, Madonna tried to rewrite the script, but the critics were not impressed and the film, released in 2000, was a disappointment at the box office. One song from the soundtrack, "American Pie," however, became a hit. Madonna was also in the process of recording her eighth studio album, titled simply *Music*, which, with its "pop melodies and electronic funk pop,"[13] was meant to be "the sound of the future," its disco, dance-oriented leanings swirled into a stylized electronica.

As she greeted the millennium, Madonna could take pride and satisfaction in having not only rescued her career from its downward 1990s spiral but in coming back out on top, with one successful film, two new albums, and five Grammy awards to show for it. She had triumphed once again, and, moving into her forties, she had retained her place as America's top pop idol. Fame and fortune were hers, and she seemed to have everything— except a happy love life.

GUY RITCHIE

She became more serious about moving to England, where she had always been a huge star and had many fans. Perhaps, too, the stalker episode had made her nervous now that she had a daughter to protect. She enlisted the help of her friend, Trudie Styler, wife of the singer Sting, who lived in a beautiful old British mansion on 52 acres in Wiltshire, England. Trudie in fact had invited Madonna to a dinner party one night in the summer of 1998, ostensibly to introduce her to a pair of filmmakers who were looking for a company like Madonna's Maverick Records to record the soundtrack of their new film, *Lock, Stock and Two Smoking Barrels*. One of the pair was Guy Ritchie, a 30-year-old, blond, athletic-looking guy who caught Madonna's eye immediately. Indeed, she reported having the same sudden realization about him that she'd had on first seeing Sean Penn, that this might be the man she would marry.[14] She said she went all "wobbly-bonkers." "My head didn't just turn, my head spun round on my body. I was taken by his confidence. He was very sort of cocky but in a self-aware way."[15]

He, like Andy Bird, was 10 years younger than Madonna. Born in England in 1968, he grew up in West London and in a seventeenth-century manor house in Shrewsbury, England. Guy Ritchie came from a long line of military men. His father, John Ritchie, and grandfather, Major Stewart Ritchie, were members of the Seaforth Highlanders, a division of the British Army. His great-grandfather, Major-General Sir William Ritchie, had been with the Indian Army. There were links to the Scottish gentry, and on his paternal grandmother's side, he has some (quite distant) connections with the late Princess of Wales, Diana, and with Winston Churchill. His mother, Amber, is a beautiful woman, a former model who divorced John Ritchie when Guy was five to become Lady Leighton as the wife of Sir Michael Leighton.[16]

It was naturally thought that Guy would follow in the footsteps of the family's distinguished military men, but he had other ideas. He was dyslexic and did not do well in school, expelled from one private school for playing hooky and having a girl in his room.[17] Leaving the academic world behind, Guy worked a series of odd jobs and bounced around for a long time in London's East End, hanging out with a motley crew. Eventually he latched on to a job with a film company in Soho where he learned the nuts and bolts of filmmaking and began writing the screenplay for his first full-length film, *Lock, Stock and Two Smoking Barrels*. The story was based on his own experiences and basically extolled the macho virtues of the lads who drank and fought and survived as denizens of the London underworld. As biographer Andrew Morton says of the film:

> Given the values of his then future bride, it is something of an irony that the movie is a hymn to homophobia and choreographed violence, a self-enclosed, amoral world in which men are macho and women absent, a kind of downmarket gentleman's smoking club in celluloid . . . the film is redeemed by a swaggering, self-deprecating sense of humor, never taking itself too seriously.[18]

Nonetheless, Morton notes, the film became something of a cult classic, capturing the mood of modern England.

When Guy and Madonna met at Sting's house in the summer of 1998, both were involved with other people, Madonna with Andy Bird and Guy with a longtime girlfriend, Rebecca Green, and later with a TV presenter, Tania Strecker. Nonetheless, they began seeing each other in the spring of 1999 and, by the end of the year, Madonna, frustrated by their long-distance romance, decided that a move to London would solidify a relationship she very much wanted to pursue. Guy Ritchie possessed enough of the bad-boy patina she favored in her men, a little of the violence she rather admired (he punched Andy Bird out at the Met Bar in their first encounter),[19] and his filmmaking career was promising. He also had an upper-class aloofness that Madonna rather liked, and he was determined not to be deterred from becoming a success at his chosen career, a quality that Madonna could relate to.[20]

She packed up Lourdes, rented a house in Notting Hill, London, put her five-year-old daughter's name on the list at Lycée Français Charles de Gaulle, and began the new millennium as a resident of the British Isles. With Guy as her escort, Madonna was well received, soon hobnobbing with society types, attending charity functions, and even dining with Prince Charles at Highgrove.[21] She acquired a British nickname, Madge, and, dubiously, a British accent. Best of all, she acquired Guy Ritchie, who moved into the Notting Hill house with her.

He was the man she would marry by the end of that year.

NOTES

1. "Madonna's Private Diaries," *Vanity Fair*, November, 1996. 174.

2. Andrew Morton. *Madonna*. (New York: St. Martin's Press, 2001). 274.

3. "Madonna's Private Diaries," 174.

4. *Ibid.*, 226.

5. Biographical material on Eva Duarte Peron is from the Wikipedia "Eva Peron" entry on http://en.wikipedia.org (accessed September 23, 2006).

6. "Madonna's Private Diaries," 223.

7. *Ibid.*, 226.

8. *Ibid.*, 228.

9. *Ibid.*

10. *Ibid.*

11. J. Randy Taraborrelli. *Madonna: An Intimate Biography*. (New York: Berkley Books/Simon & Schuster, 2002). 308.

12. Barbara Victor. *Goddess: Inside Madonna*. (New York: Cliff Street Books/HarperCollins, 2001). 348–349.

13. Taraborrelli, 359–360.

14. Victor, 351–352.

15. Morton, 301.

16. Morton, 303; Taraborrelli, 340.

17. Morton, 304.

18. *Ibid.*, 305.

19. Taraborrelli, 348.

20. *Ibid.*, 344–46.

21. Morton, 308.

Chapter 8

MADONNA, THE PROFESSORS, AND THE FEMINISTS

Despite the negative press and public censure she had endured during the 1990s for her career move into ever more outrageous and sexually oriented material, Madonna was becoming an exalted star on the unlikely stage of academia, where professors had launched a major industry of courses and scholarly articles about Madonna as a "postmodern icon."

The turmoil of new theory imported from Europe and the culture wars of ideology were bringing huge changes to the American academic world and the college curriculum. Whole departments devoted to popular culture and media studies emerged, women's studies came into its own, and literature departments were abuzz with deconstruction and cultural theory. The feminists in academia and elsewhere had already had a lot to say about Madonna, both pro and con. Now the faculty in traditional English, sociology, and communications departments were also publishing articles in scholarly journals about her. Although as a pop star performer she was hardly the usual subject for scholars' heavily footnoted works, Madonna seemed to illustrate extremely well what was happening on the embattled cultural ramparts of late twentieth-century America.

It was not only her transgressive behavior, breaking down barriers about what could be shown and said in the media world, but her rapidly changing image, her quick appropriation of cultural trends, and her power over the stream of images pouring out of MTV and other media—to say nothing of her music—that were a perfect example of the whole theory of postmodernism the academic world was suddenly so immersed in. She was viewed as a veritable postmodern icon, a force field embodying those qualities of playful pastiche, parody, indeterminacy, and commodified image said to be characteristic of our postmodern age. If postmodernism is preoccupied "with the signifier [the word or object] rather than the signified [meaning], with participation, performance, and happening rather than with an authoritative and finished art object, with surface appearances rather than roots," as David Harvey claims in *The Condition of Postmodernism*,[1] Madonna certainly fit the description and then some.

Her chameleon persona, her gender-bending role play, her imitation and parody of glamorous Hollywood stars, her playful inversions of Madonna/Whore imagery, and her allusive sampling of styles and genres positioned her as an avatar of postmodernism for the new professor practitioners of cultural, gender, and media studies. During the early 1990s, classes with titles like "Race, Culture, and Madonna" were all over college curriculums. Whether or not Madonna was aware of it (and there's some evidence that she was), she had become a prime subject for scholarly inquiry; her wannabe followers, now in college, were still following her, now writing papers about her as well as buying her albums and pushing them to the top of the charts.

What is interesting about all the scholarly investigation of Madonna is how well she exemplified the cultural moment, as if she picked up on the *zeitgeist* before anyone else (and she is supremely good at trend-spotting) and made it her own, handing it back in fascinating ways. From her ragtag fashions and vogue-ing, drag queen ensembles to her danceable mix of music incorporating techno, hip hop, rap, and disco, Madonna brilliantly managed to capture the spirit of the times and play the postmodern for all it was worth.

As the French scholar Jean Baudrillard says of Madonna: "She does obtain a mix, a multiculturalism, and also a questioning of sexual difference, by shuffling the cards, all the cards. Maybe that's what post-modern means," the "possibility to dislocate."[2] E. Ann Kaplan, director of the Humanities Institute at the State University of New York-Stony Brook and author of *Rocking Around the Clock: Music Television, Postmodernism and Consumer Culture*, calls it the "Madonna phenomenon," saying that Madonna's masks and masquerades actually problematize "the bourgeois illusion of 'real' individual ordered selves (there is nothing *but* masks)"[3] and "exemplifies the politics of the signifier," disrupting conventional meanings with her chameleon performance of gender-dissolving sexual categories.[4]

Cathy Schwichtenberg, a University of Georgia professor and editor of the scholarly volume, *The Madonna Connection: Representational Politics, Subcultural Identities, and Cultural Theory*, sees Madonna as deconstructing and fragmenting cultural categories, particularly gender boundaries,[5] pushing the envelope "toward the postmodern possibilities of multifaceted alliances."[6] "To entertain multiple styles, surfaces, sexualities, and identities," as Madonna does, "may move us from the margin to the center in coalitional acts of resistance and disruption," Schwichtenberg concludes.[7]

In her book, *Madonna, Bawdy and Soul*, Canadian feminist Karlene Faith says that a good reason for Madonna's popularity might be the very "amorphousness, layering or multiplicity" of her image. Anchored in the "possibility of power and control," this image is alluring, "given the fractured, fragmented, disempowered, and resistant identities that characterize the postmodern age."[8] In Madonna's embrace of a variety of ethnic, racial, and gender groups, she "crosses many cultural borders," becoming "whomever she represents in any given moment"—and in the next moment, contradicting it.[9]

Georges-Claude Guilbert, author of *Madonna as Postmodern Myth* and a professor at the University of Rouen in France, suggests that Madonna is "America's mirror," reflecting our obsession with celebrity and endorsing our values of hard work as well as our dreams of success. As a self-made star, Madonna is "her own fairy godmother,"[10] he says. By reinventing herself, she reinvents America "at every moment."[11]

"Madonna is her contradictions," critic Douglas Kellner claims in his essay, "Madonna, Fashion, and Identity." While she subverts conventional codes of identity, sexuality, and gender, Madonna at the same time reinforces them by speaking to a consumer society's norms, constructing identity in terms of fashion and image. "Grasping this contradiction is the key to Madonna's effects," Kellner says. For example, the "Boy Toy" "un-chastity" belt Madonna wears in her *Lucky Star* video can be interpreted two ways: she's a plaything for men, but her toys are boys. It's this kind of "ambiguity, irony, and humor" that have made her a focus of academic analysis, he says. "Her breaking of rules has progressive elements in that it goes against ruling gender, sex, fashion, and racial hierarchies, and her message that identity is something that everyone can have and must construct for themselves is also appealing," Kellner concludes.[12]

Long before Madonna came on the scene, another French theorist, Guy Debord, wrote a prophetic book, *Society of the Spectacle*, describing the social transformations that eventually prepared the way for a media phenomenon like Madonna. In the book, he claims that "Everything that was directly lived has moved away into representation,"[13] as media technology—television, film, and now the Internet and DVD—has reorganized our world and our consciousness, changing the real world "into simple images" that eventually seem to "become real beings."[14] Our postmodern lives, in short, have become "mediated by images."[15] The spectacle becomes "the historical movement in which we are caught," our world view.[16] And, in the society of the spectacle, the celebrity becomes:

> . . . the spectacular representation of a living human being . . . embodying the image of a possible role. . . . Being a star means specializing in the *seemingly lived*; the star is the object of identification with the shallow-seeming life that has to compensate for the fragmented productive specializations which are actually lived. Celebrities exist to act out various styles of living and viewing society—unfettered, free to express themselves *globally*.[17]

Although Debord, a Marxist, goes on to connect the society of the spectacle with the workings of capitalism (as indeed other postmodern theorists have), showing how "the world of the commodity" dominates the spectacle, his analysis of what was happening as media technology increasingly colonized the world is prophetic. It offers a rationale for our ongoing obsession with celebrity as well as an uncanny prediction of a phenomenon like Madonna. Whether or not she ever read Debord, she read the cultural climate perfectly and acted it out for us, whether as Boy Toy, drag queen, Hollywood star, disco bimbo, dominatrix, or coy schoolgirl. As one of the first female singers on MTV, her early videos enshrined Madonna as queen of the society of spectacle and her music as a worldwide sensation.

Indeed, video (and now DVD) "can lay some claim to being postmodernism's most distinctive new medium,"[18] according to Frederic Jameson, the scholar guru of postmodernism and author of *Postmodernism, or, The Cultural Logic of Late Capitalism* (xv). In a chapter about the impact of video, he speaks of how it exemplifies postmodernism's "pure and random play of signifiers," ceaselessly reshuffling "the fragments of preexistent texts, the building blocks of older cultural and social production, in some new and heightened *bricolage* [italics mine]."[19] Dissolving old categories, problematizing meaning, and playing games with sexual stereotypes, Madonna's videos reshuffle and repackage conventional ideas about men, women, love, sex, and about a way of life that has become increasingly a matter of surface, sound, and image.

Very postmodern, as Jameson points out, noting that even in advertising, brand names have been "transformed into an image, a sign or emblem which carries the memory of a whole tradition of earlier advertisements within itself in a well-nigh intertextual way."[20] Like a brand name or logo,

Madonna too has transformed herself into a commodified, iconic image that includes allusions to earlier performers and to her own performances in an intertextual way. Yet "she is neither a text nor a person, but a set of meanings in process," as John Fiske remarks in *Understanding Popular Culture*.[21]

If, as Guy Debord says, "The spectacle is the other side of money,"[22] Madonna's staging of the spectacle enshrines desire and capitalizes on consumerism. Madonna celebrates abundance, selling not only her "brand" and her music, but an image that says we too can have it all, the goods and the freedom to enjoy them any way we want. Her *Material Girl* video, for example, in its replay of Marilyn Monroe's image and its accent on sex and money, speaks volumes about the way capitalism's pervasive appropriation of image makes commodities visible—cars, I-Pods, lipstick, lifestyles—and makes us conscious of desire for them. Madonna herself is not shy about admitting to materialism. She told one writer she wanted "just the best of everything there is to have."[23]

Postmodernism has also opened up a split between so-called high culture and low culture, exalting the low, the popular, and the street as the authentic milieu. Madonna understands this well, running the risk of being condemned and disliked for her deliberate impersonations of the slut, the prostitute, and the stripper. Her claim to be a child of the working class and to have lived on the streets of New York eating out of dumpsters, while not entirely true, gives her street cred among her fans and shields her from any accusation of elitism. She cultivates the music of the streets and subcultures—rap, hip hop—and incorporates the street sports of skateboarding and break dancing into her concert tours and videos. But what upsets some of her fans and many feminists is her transgressive, in-your-face sexuality. Certainly the *Sex* book of 1992 outraged—and captivated—many with its graphic depiction of S&M, lesbianism, bisexuality, and female eroticism.

One of Madonna's most outspoken defenders against those who have condemned the pop star's frank female sexuality is Camille Paglia, a professor of humanities at Philadelphia's University of the Arts. "I'm a dyed-in-the-wool, true-blue Madonna fan," she confesses.[24] All those provocative, sexually charged videos and songs, with Madonna writhing in black bustiers and kissing statues of saints in church? According to Paglia, the world of "parched, pinched, word-drunk Anglo-Saxon feminism" doesn't get it: Madonna should be lauded for teaching "young women to be fully female and sexual while still exercising control over their lives."[25] Madonna is, says Paglia, "a complex modern woman" who explores "the problems and tensions of being an ambitious woman today,"[26] someone who has the guts to confront the patriarchal system with uninhibited female sensuality and eroticism.

Feminists don't all agree with her on this point, many seeing Madonna instead as capitalizing on stereotypes of female seductiveness and oppression and setting a bad example for young women. Feminism itself is divided, not only about Madonna but about what feminism represents. One thing is clear: Madonna has inspired reams of feminist commentary. And the feminists have taken Madonna severely to task, not just for the *Sex* book, but for her entire sexual persona, seeing her as endorsing woman-as-sex-object and slave to men. They say her sexually saturated image, her sexual shock tactics, and her display of her body make her an antifeminist, inviting the male gaze and endorsing the same old patriarchal codes of woman as seductress. She's been called a "ho," a bimbo, a corrupting influence, a step backward for womankind. Yet while feminism itself is split into various camps and the word "feminist" has acquired negative connotations (man-hating, radical, shrewish), scholars like Camille Paglia see Madonna's pleasure in her own sexuality and her seeming independence from men as signs of "the future of feminism."[27] "Playing with the outlaw personae of prostitute and dominatrix, Madonna has made a major contribution to the history of women. She has rejoined and healed the split halves of woman: Mary, the Blessed Virgin and holy mother, and Mary Magdelene, the harlot," Paglia says.[28] Another writer, Barbara Victor, claims that Madonna is "the patron saint of the trailer-park feminist," validating the lives of women excluded from mainstream feminism.[29] Others applaud Madonna for exposing the codes of femininity as mere masquerade. Drawing on Judith Butler's *Gender Trouble*, Cathy Schwichtenberg in "Madonna's Postmodern Feminism" says that Madonna "bares the devices of femininity, thereby asserting that femininity is a device." Madonna deconstructs gender to show it as but "an overplay of style."[30] In Butler's terms, Madonna reveals gender as "performative—that is, constituting the identity it is purported to be. In this sense, gender is always a doing."[31]

What does the general public think of Madonna? Certainly the overwhelming success of her music, videos/DVDs, concert tours, and sales speaks volumes about her popularity and fan base, as do the more than 40 Web sites on the Internet devoted exclusively to Madonna news, gossip, photographs, and trivia. Books about Madonna—her life, her look, her music—abound. And you don't sell out an international tour months before you go on the road, as Madonna does, unless there are legions of fans ready to pay $95 and up for a ticket in Japan, Australia, Israel, France, Italy, England, and Russia, as well as the United States.

Still, the public definitely has a love-hate relationship with Madonna. Her publicist, Liz Rosenberg, says that actually means more press since "everyone ha[s] to take a stance on Madonna. I love when people really hate Madonna—Madonna does, too. She'd rather that than apathy."[32] There's even an *I Hate Madonna Handbook*. Music critics have not been kind. One, Martha Bayles, author of *Hole in Our Soul: The Loss of Beauty and Meaning in American Popular Music*, sees Madonna as mainly "a selfish, manipulative person" whose "'art' is largely a matter of acting out unresolved psychosexual conflicts" in "fizzy, upbeat 'dance music.'"[33] In a 1990s scholarly article about Madonna-haters, three professors used a newspaper poll and a set of college student responses to Madonna videos to count the ways: (1) Madonna as "the lowest form of aesthetic culture" ("commercial" and "shallow" among other things); (2) Madonna as "social disease," corrupting children; (3) Madonna as "the female grotesque" man-eating vampire; and (4) Madonna as antifeminist.[34]

> Described as "shallow, kitschy pop entertainment," "pure, commercial Hokum," "gleaming and superficial," and "manipulative," Madonna signifies the low-Other of popular art, the media package that demonstrates the power of the culture industry to successfully commodify a performer with no talent.[35]

Respondents saw Madonna as "a source of moral contagion"[36] to children and families and as anti-Christian for wearing crucifixes as jewelry. The fact that Madonna seems actually to enjoy her own sexuality was also condemned. Horror of patriarchal horrors, maybe she doesn't need men at all. Or, she's just a throwback bimbo, playing the usual seductress games and luring men to their ruin. The authors of the Madonna-hater study suggest that a "patriarchal framework" and discourse remain strong enough in our culture to condition many people's response to an iconoclast like Madonna.[37]

One fan who has been a loyal defender of Madonna against her critics is gossip columnist Liz Smith who writes for *The New York Post*. "Her misdeeds," Smith writes in her autobiography, *Natural Blonde*, referring to Madonna's *Sex* book and her expletive-peppered David Letterman appearance, "were so blown out of proportion by most of the media that I felt compelled, if not to defend her, then to at least present a more balanced view."[38] Smith calls Madonna "a marketing genius," with a real artist's imagination and daring."[39] "Madonna once phoned my office at the height of her 'unpopularity' in the wake of the *Sex* book and her *Body of Evidence* movie," Smith writes. "'It's Madonna,' she said, getting right to the point. 'I just wanted to call and say thanks for the support you've given me. I know you get a lot of shit because of it.'"[40] Madonna phones Liz Smith directly when she's about to make big news; she called her from Budapest while filming *Evita* to tell her she was pregnant.[41]

During the furor over Madonna's appearance wearing a crown of thorns on a cross during her 2006 *Confessions on a Dance Floor* tour, Smith wrote a whole column in the *Post* to defend her. "Forget the crucifix. No, really," Smith wrote. "There is more to M's work than meets the eye," describing the controversial scene as Madonna's way of dramatizing her concern about the spread of AIDS in Africa.[42] Madonna says, "I love Liz Smith because she has balls, like me!"[43]

A surprise defender of Madonna is Norman Mailer, who called her "our greatest living female artist" in an essay for *Esquire* magazine in August of 1994, just at the time when her career was bottoming out over the *Sex* book and her S&M exploits on video. He said she was unusual among celebrities for choosing film roles that didn't boost her status, and he compared her to Andy Warhol who also challenged cultural convention and ideology.[44]

NOTES

1. David Harvey. *The Condition of Postmodernity*. (Oxford: Basil Blackwell, Ltd., 1990), 53.

2. Jean Baudrillard. "Madonna Deconnection." in *Madonna: erotisme et pouvoir*. ed. Michel Dion. (Paris: Editions Kinme, 1994), 29–30.

3. E. Ann Kaplan. "Madonna Politics: Perversion, Repression, or Subversion? Or Masks and/as Mastery." in *The Madonna Connection: Representational Politics, Subcultural Identities, and Cultural Theory*. ed. Cathy Schwichtenberg, (Boulder: Westview Press,1993), 150.

4. Kaplan, 157.

5. Cathy Schwichtenberg. "Madonna's Postmodern Feminism: Bringing the Margins to the Center." in *The Madonna Connection: Representational Politics, Subcultural Identities, and Cultural Theory*. ed. Cathy Schwichtenberg. (Boulder: Westview Press, 1993), 132.

6. *Ibid.*, 140.

7. *Ibid.*, 141.

8. Karlene Faith. *Madonna,Bawdy and Soul*. (Toronto: University of Toronto Press, 1997), 96.

9. *Ibid.*, 95.

10. Georges-Claude Guilbert. *Madonna as Postmodern Myth*. (Jefferson, N.C.: McFarland & Company, 2002), 152.

11. *Ibid.*, 162.

12. Douglas Kellner. "Madonna, Fashion, and Identity." in *On Fashion*, ed. Shari Benstock and Suzanne Ferriss. (New Brunswick: Rutgers University Press, 1994). 159–182.

13. Guy Debord. *Society of the Spectacle*. (Detroit: Black and Red, 1983), 1.

14. *Ibid.*, 18.

15. *Ibid.*, 4.

16. *Ibid.*, 15.

17. *Ibid.*, 60.

18. Frederic Jameson. *Postmodernism, or, The Cultural Logic of Late Capitalism*. (Durham, N.C.: Duke University Press, 1991), xv.

19. *Ibid.*, 96. The French word, "bricolage," was used by Jacques Derrida to mean the mix of new modes of perception..

20. *Ibid.*, 85.

21. John Fiske. *Understanding Popular Culture*. (Winchester, Mass.: Unwin Hyman, 1989). 124.

22. Debord, 49.

23. J. Randy Taraborrelli. *Madonna: An Intimate Biography*. (Berkley Books/Simon & Schuster, 2001). 417.

24. Camille Paglia. *Sex, Art, and American Culture*. (New York: Vintage Books, 1993), 8.

25. *Ibid.*, 4.

26. *Ibid.*, 13.

27. *Ibid.*, 5.

28. *Ibid.*, 11.

29. Barbara Victor. *Goddess: Inside Madonna*. (New York: Cliff Street Books/HarperCollins, 2001). 103.

30. Schwichtenberg, 134.

31. Judith Butler. *Gender Trouble: Feminism and the Subversion of Identity*. (New York: Routledge, 1990). 25.

32. Quoted by Maureen Orth. "Madonna in Wonderland." *Vanity Fair*. October 1991. 298.

33. Martha Bayles. *Hole in Our Soul: The Loss of Beauty and Meaning in American Popular Music*. (New York: The Free Press/Macmillan, Inc., 1994). 335, 334.

34. Laurie Schulze, Anne Barton White, and Jane D. Brown. "A Sacred Monster in Her Prime": Audience Construction of Madonna as Low-Other." in *The Madonna Connection: Representational Politics, Subcultural Identities, and Cultural Theory*, ed. Cathy Schwichtenberg. (Boulder: Westview Press, 1993). 17.

35. *Ibid.*, 18.

36. *Ibid.*, 22.

37. *Ibid.*, 31.

38. Liz Smith. *Natural Blonde*. (New York: Hyperion, 2000). 429.

39. *Ibid.*, 429–430.

40. *Ibid.*, 430.

41. Liz Smith, "Listen, Look Beyond Crucifix," *The New York Post* online edition, 25 May 2006, www.nypost.com/gossip/liz.

42. Smith, *Natural Blonde*, 429.

43. Smith. "Listen, Look Beyond Crucifix."

44. "Mailer on Madonna." *Esquire*. August 1994.

Chapter 9

LIFE AMONG
THE ENGLISH ROSES

The year 2000, the beginning of a new millennium, was a brand-new beginning too for Madonna. She had found the man she loved and had moved to a new country to begin the next chapter of her life. Her new and eighth studio album, *Music*, a collection of dance and pop music, co-written with Mirwais Ahmadzai, a French techno musician, was released in September and was her first album since *Like A Prayer* in 1989 to go to Number One. The track included "I Deserve It," with the line, "This guy was made for me" (on stage, she called Ritchie "the coolest guy in the universe," a comment she had also once made about Sean Penn).[1] Her new movie, *The Next Best Thing*, starring Madonna as a California yoga instructor opposite the British actor Rupert Everett, was released that fall as well, although to less than favorable reviews. Madonna had been presented with her fifth Grammy award that spring for "Beautiful Stranger," the song she wrote for *Austin Powers: The Spy Who Shagged Me*. And, by the end of 2000, Madonna would not only have a new husband but a new baby.

Now dubbed "Her Madge-esty" by the British tabloids, Madonna took to life in her adopted country well, especially with Guy Ritchie at her side. They were living in Notting Hill in London in a house Madonna had rented, and the relationship improved, despite many ups and downs. For Madonna, being in the same country—and the same house—with Guy was much better than trying to keep the relationship going across the Atlantic Ocean and a whole continent. Yet Guy could be distant. He was intent on making it in film and often was unavailable when Madonna, used to being in control, wanted to be with him. Madonna had always had a bad habit of obsessively phoning her boyfriends, perhaps an indication of a basic insecurity about her men. Trudy Styler told her to cut it out with Guy, that she was driving him away. He was just as serious about his career as Madonna was about hers and needed time and space to pursue his work. Perhaps this made him more attractive to Madonna, used to having what she wanted whenever she wanted it. She stopped all the phoning.

She relied on Trudy for advice about how to fit into the British lifestyle and became friends with Stella McCartney, the designer (and daughter of Paul) who would later design her wedding dress. Gwyneth Paltrow, a good friend from the States, was in town occasionally, and even Carlos Leon came to London to visit his daughter.

ROCCO JOHN RITCHIE

In February, Madonna confirmed the tabloid rumors that she was pregnant, the baby due in September. Guy, it was said, was somewhat uneasy about the pregnancy and the commitment this seemed to imply. His family was worried that Guy's nascent film career might be affected by having a child, even suggesting that Madonna had deliberately gotten pregnant. He was working on a new film, *Snatch*, due in September as well. As luck would have it, both the baby and the film were produced on time.

Madonna had decided to have the baby in Los Angeles where she had recently bought and was renovating Diane Keaton's former house on Roxbury Drive in Beverly Hills. She returned in the summer to her Los Feliz house (soon to be sold) in Los Angeles to await the birth. Gwyneth Paltrow gave her a baby shower, and the nursery was ready. On the night of August 10, alone at home, she suddenly began to hemorrhage. Guy was nearby playing poker with Brad Pitt (who was starring in *Snatch*).[2] Madonna quickly called her doctor and her future husband and was whisked away in an ambulance to Cedars-Sinai Medical Center where Guy, following the ambulance, checked her in under the name of his sister, Tabitha. Madonna, losing blood, was found to be suffering what technically is known as placenta previa, a detached placenta that would mean the baby was being deprived of oxygen. Her life was in danger as well.

Doctors decided on an emergency cesarean delivery, and Rocco John Ritchie was born in the wee hours of August 11, 2000, three weeks early, weighing 6 pounds 3 ounces.[3] He was jaundiced and had breathing difficulties and was placed in an incubator. But he was in his exhausted mother's arms 12 hours later and friends said that his father, Guy Ritchie, chastened by the experience of nearly losing both the baby and Madonna, was "over the moon" about the birth.[4] Madonna said she was thrilled that Lourdes now had a baby brother. Rocco had to stay in the hospital for five more days, but was allowed to come home on his mother's birthday August 16, a very nice 42nd birthday present for Madonna.

Indeed, Rocco's birth changed everything about the relationship between Madonna and Guy. The baby thrived and so did his mother and father, who soon announced that they would marry, Guy presenting Madonna with a ring when she got home from the hospital. Tony Ciccone was delighted to hear about the wedding plans and made a special trip with his wife that September to see the new baby. Guy's family were reportedly not so delighted about the wedding at first, fearing their 32-year-old son and a 42-year-old pop star might not be the best match.

Madonna was determined to regain her figure and take on new motherhood as her well-toned self, and she did. Her regular exercise regimen—running, lifting weights, and working out—paid off. She got her figure back quickly and a month after Rocco's birth, she managed to give a party for 600 people in a Los Angeles club to celebrate the release of her new album, *Music.* Looking svelte and wearing a black tee shirt advertising Guy's new movie, *Snatch,* she mingled with her celebrity guests but left early with Guy to go home to Rocco.[5]

WEDDING BELLS

Madonna had married Sean Penn on her birthday, August 16, but she picked her new future husband's birthday, December 22, for this wedding day. She began making plans for a ceremony that would be nothing like the paparazzi frenzy her wedding to Sean had been. But first, little baby Rocco had to be christened. Since the wedding was to be in Scotland at a remote castle in Dornoch, Madonna decided that the christening for Rocco would be held the day before the wedding on December 21 at the cathedral in Dornoch. While the location in Scotland was chosen to honor Guy's heritage, Madonna also wanted to marry in the Church of Scotland where her previous divorce would not be an issue.

Madonna asked her friend Stella McCartney to design her wedding dress, an ivory duchesse satin strapless gown with a train and corseted bodice that gave her an hourglass figure ("a real boob squisher!," Madonna told *Vogue* magazine later[6]). Worn with an antique lace veil, the dress cost a reported $30,000. She would wear the diamond Cartier tiara that Grace Kelly wore to her daughter Caroline's wedding and a 27-carat diamond cross around her neck, on loan from Harry Winston. On her feet were a pair of Jimmy Choo shoes. The entire wedding cost approximately $1.7 million, and Madonna reportedly paid for the whole thing.[7]

For his christening, little Rocco would be dressed in a cream silk gown designed by another friend, Donatella Versace (again, a costly creation at $15,000). He was bundled up in a warm suit with a bunny hat for the ride to the cathedral. There were, however, no photographs released to the press of Madonna or Rocco in all this finery. Madonna had ordered a complete press blackout and she succeeded, except for one photo she allowed as they left the christening ceremony.[8]

The Reverend Susan Brown, the minister in charge of the Dornoch cathedral, presided over the christening, with Trudy Styler as Rocco's godmother. Trudy's husband, Sting, sang "Ave Maria" for the ceremony. Guy Oseary, who had been Madonna's partner in Maverick Records and would soon be her new manager, was Rocco's godfather. Madonna wore a beautiful off-white silk coat and a black veil with her hair in a twist, a very *Evita* look. Assembled for the christening were Madonna's father and stepmother and Guy's father John with his second wife, Shireen. Guy's mother, Lady Amber Leighton, was also in attendance as were Gwyneth Paltrow and other friends. Baby Rocco behaved beautifully and didn't cry, although a few others, including his father, did have tears in their eyes, according to witnesses. The Rev. Brown carried Rocco in her arms down the aisle to show him off to the congregation.[9] Outside, local residents cheered Madonna, Guy, and Rocco as they emerged from the cathedral and made their way back to Skibo Castle where the wedding would be held a day later and where guests were already arriving.

Some of the guests were family, like Madonna's little sister Melanie and her husband Joe Henry and her brother Christopher, who were the only ones of her siblings she invited to the wedding. Members of Guy's family were also staying at the nineteenth-century castle, which has 21 bedrooms and more in lodges around its 7,500 acres of forests and moors. It had been bought and restored by Andrew Carnegie, the American steel magnate, in 1898 and later sold to owners who renovated the castle as a resort. Other guests staying there included Donatella Versace, Stella McCartney, and Gwyneth Paltrow.[10]

The candlelight wedding ceremony on December 22 began at 6:30 P.M. in the Great Hall of the castle, with a bagpiper leading the procession. Little four-year-old Lourdes, barefoot in a long Stella McCartney ivory dress, scattered red rose petals as she walked. Stella McCartney, attired in a McCartney-designed gray pants suit, was maid of honor for Madonna, and Guy's best men were his film company partner, Mathew Vaughn (son of Robert Vaughn, star of the TV series, *The Man from U.N.C.L.E.*), and Piers Adam, a friend and nightclub owner. Madonna came down the aisle on the arm of her father Tony to take her vows. Guy was wearing a navy and green Hunting Mackintosh kilt (Rocco, in the front row with his nanny, wore a kilt to match). The Reverend Susan Brown presided over the wedding ceremony, which included vows that Madonna and Guy had written, including "cherish, honor, and delight in family," and the couple exchanged platinum wedding rings.[11] There were just 55 guests to witness the ceremony, including Rupert Everett, Madonna's co-star in *The Next Best Thing*, Alek Keshishian, the designer Jean-Paul Gaultier, some of Madonna's friends including Ingrid Casares and Debi Mazur, and many of Guy's buddies.

Outside, photographers and television crews hoping to catch a glimpse of the festivities shivered in the cold December night, as crews of security men kept them at a distance and frustrated their attempts to photograph the event. Inside, in the Skibo Castle drawing room, guests sipped champagne and toasted the new bride and groom, then sat down to a wedding dinner of Scottish haggis, roast beef, salmon, and lobster, serenaded by a Scottish band and warmed by the fires in the many castle fireplaces. For dessert, there was a wedding cake in the shape of a piano, a gift from Sting and Trudy Styler.[12]

Madonna threw her bouquet—and Lourdes caught it. Then the party moved on to a disco in the basement of the castle where a disc jockey from Miami, Tracy Young, filled the room with Madonna music. Madonna had by this time changed her clothes twice, out of her wedding dress and into a Jean-Paul Gaultier ensemble for dinner and then into a Versace ivory pantsuit for the party. She and Guy slipped away at dawn to their bridal suite in the castle. They would spend a brief honeymoon and Christmas at the Lake House home of Trudy and Sting in Wiltshire, where they first met.[13]

HER MADG-ESTY

A married woman once again and the mother of two, Madonna must have greeted the new year with a sense of profound fulfillment. At last she had the family she had longed for, a new husband, and two beautiful children. While Madonna seemed to embrace the domesticity of it all, she and Guy never lost sight of their respective careers. Madonna was planning her *Drowned World* tour, her first in eight years, and Guy was considering a remake of Lina Wertmuller's *Swept Away*, to star—who else?—Madonna.

She had bought a London house in the West End just a week before the wedding where her new family would settle in the new year. Madonna had reportedly paid $10 million for the eighteenth-century Georgian mansion with eight bedrooms. In June 2000, she had sold her Miami house in Biscayne Bay (for $7.5 million)[14] and was still in the process of renovating the Los Angeles house she bought from her friend Diane Keaton where the couple and their children would eventually spend much of their time. There would be one more house to come, Ashcombe House near Stonehenge in England, the former home of Cecil Beaton, the noted photographer. "I see England as my home," she told Hamish Bowles in an interview for *Vogue* magazine. "I love England and want to be here and not in America."[15] Bowles comments that Madonna "has the air of an Edwardian dollar princess—the moneyed American belles who were married off to impecunious British nobles in the golden age—and the fragile beauty and substantial real estate to match."[16]

The seventeenth-century Ashcombe estate encompasses 1,000 acres of fields and hills near the ancient Druid ruins at Stonehenge. Replete with horses and stables, partridges and pheasants, chickens and farmland, antiques and servants, it speaks of landed gentry and a leisurely country life. "Who would have thunk it?," Madonna says. "The last thing I thought I would do is marry some laddish, shooting, pubgoing nature lover—and the last thing he thought he was going to do was marry some cheeky girl from the Midwest who doesn't take no for an answer!"[17]

When the Ritchies bought the estate, the main house was long gone, but they turned a dairy house and stable on the property into beautiful, liveable space, "classic England meets pampered Hollywood" with slipcovered sofas and sporting prints as well as state-of-the-art sound systems."[18] Madonna says she loves entertaining friends here. Ashcombe, she says, "is one of those places that are very conducive to bringing a group down. I'd love to do it more, but it's unbelievably complicated for my friends to each have a free weekend on the same weekend!"[19] Madonna says she likes to get her guests involved in putting on short plays and performances as weekend entertainment.

She has taken up riding (and an upper-class British accent) at Ashcombe and, with a nod to her husband's interests, learned to shoot and fish. In August 2005, just after her 47th birthday, Madonna took a spill riding her horse at Ashcombe, and ended up breaking nine bones, including three ribs, her hand, and her collarbone (headlines read: "Madonna Falls Off Her High Horse"). Amazingly, but not without a lot of physical therapy, she recovered quickly enough to go through the rigorous preparations that winter for her next tour, *Confessions on a Dance Floor* (she also had a hernia operation in February 2006). She soon got back in the saddle and went riding on West 53rd Street in New York City with David Letterman that October for a segment on his show, her dignified performance on horseback a far cry from her f-word outbursts on the show 10 years earlier.

Guy began filming in the fall of 2001 for *Swept Away*, in which Madonna would play a rich Italian socialite, Rafaella, marooned on a desert island with a sailor who turns her into his slave. Lina Wertmuller's original 1975 film explored gender boundaries and women's oppression, but Ritchie's version of the film, released in 2002, and Madonna's acting skills were roundly panned by the critics. Madonna in fact received yet another "Worst Actress" Razzie/Golden Raspberry Award for her efforts. Although she did appear in a short marketing film for BMW, *The Hire: Star*, in 2001, directed by Guy Ritchie, and did a cameo as a fencing instructor in the James Bond film, *Die Another Day* (for which she also recorded the title song), Madonna has not appeared in film for the past four years. She told *Vanity Fair*, "To me, the whole process of being a brushstroke in someone else's painting is a little difficult. I'm used to being in charge of everything."[20] Indeed, her most successful films have been those in which she gets to play herself, as in *Desperately Seeking Susan*, or a personality she admires, like *Evita*.

ON TOUR

Madonna's *Drowned World* tour, her first in eight years, took her far from home in the spring and summer of 2001, performing in the United States and Europe. Nonetheless, the tour, her first as wife and mother, was a sellout. Undoubtedly, fans wanted to see if being "Mrs. Ritchie" had changed her. They were not disappointed. The show had Madonna stamped all over it, from its dark, gothic scenarios to its theatrical, elaborate costumes to the background videos that have now become a trademark in a Madonna concert. Walking on stage wearing a Scottish plaid skirt and a black tee shirt with "mother" on the front (and "fucker" on the back), she gave her fans a good look at both the old and the new Madonna. One new song, "What It Feels Like for a Girl," written by Madonna when she was pregnant with Rocco, was banned by MTV when it came out in a video directed by Guy Ritchie as too graphically violent. As with its ban on the "Justify My Love" video, MTV's ban on *What It Feels Like for a Girl* did not by any means keep the video from selling out to the public.

Guy and the children accompanied Madonna to Paris on tour, but naturally could not be waiting in the wings at every performance across Europe. Indeed Rocco, making his first trip to the Continent, was only 10 months old that June. Madonna was beginning to get a taste of the classic female conflict between career and family. Lourdes, she told Ellen Degeneres on TV recently, is always begging her to stay home. Madonna's new documentary, *I've Got a Secret to Tell You*, filmed during her 2004 *Re-Invention* tour, includes a good deal of footage of Lourdes and Rocco playing happily together and with their parents. But at one point in the documentary, Lourdes, who talks and bats her eyelashes just like her mother, says somewhat wistfully, "My mom is very busy," but "I'm happy to get my mom back" when she's done with the tour.

Lourdes is already very much into fashion and even has her own stylist. Spotted this spring in Los Angeles by *New York Post* reporter Danico Lo, Lourdes was "dressed to the nines" (also her age at the time), "channeling mom's Danceteria days" in "Converse All Stars, green knee-highs, a retro 80s-style denim skirt and a striped henley," and swinging her flower-print pocketbook like a pro:

> Madonna's push-the-envelope genes and rebellious streak are in her blood, and their mother-daughter shopping trips to Harvey Nicks and Harrods have fostered her posh fashion sense. This wee fashion plate, like mom, eschews prissy frocks in favor of pushing the limits of fashion, favors clothes from boutique Bunny London, facials at London's Eve Lom, manicures from Daniel Galvin's salon and posh department store makeup.[21]

As Lola moves into adolescence, good luck, Madonna!

Rocco, on the other hand, now a robust six-year-old, is all boy and couldn't care less about fashion, to judge from his fleeting appearances on the documentary, *I've Got a Secret to Tell You*. He is shown fishing with his father (whom he resembles), zipping down the slide at a swimming pool, and playing with boy toys like a plastic sword. He's a good straight man for his sister's knock-knock jokes and roars with laughter at them. They seem to get along well. Madonna says she's jealous of her nanny, who "gets to have all the fun" being with the children every day.

Certainly Madonna, a motherless child, must have done much soul-searching about being a good mother to Lourdes and Rocco. Although she is able to make sure her children have the best of everything, including good private schools, French lessons (she wants her children to be bilingual), comfortable homes, and excellent care, Madonna undoubtedly feels the same tug that every working mother does when she has to walk out the door and go to work. But in a 2005 interview, she said that she's very strict with her children. "I'm the disciplinarian . . . I do all the necessary stuff. Guy's the spoiler. When Daddy gets home, they're going to get chocolate." Madonna says that television, magazines, and newspapers are off limits in her household, but that Lourdes and Rocco get to watch movies on Sundays ("if they're naughty they get their movie taken away"). She also settles fights about clothing quickly: "If you're going to throw a tantrum about clothes, they're going to get taken away. So we have gotten down to one outfit."[22] Madonna boasted to *Rolling Stone* that after this interview was published, she got a letter from Dr. Benjamin Spock's wife approving of her child-raising techniques.[23]

KABBALAH

Even before she became a mother and despite her supreme air of self-confidence, Madonna always struggled with feelings of insecurity. She was searching for something else beyond the adulation and fame and wealth and began to feel the need for a deeper spiritual life. "As corny as it sounds, if I didn't have some kind of spiritual belief system, if I couldn't find a way to make sense out of the chaos in the world around me—not my personal chaos, but the chaos in the world—I would be a very depressed person."[24]

Despite her Catholic upbringing, in 1996 while pregnant with Lourdes, she became involved in a Los Angeles group exploring a branch of the Jewish faith, Kabbalah, which seemed to offer what she had been looking for. Kabbalah , an interpretation of the first five books of the Old Testament, the Torah (the Law), "explains the complexities of the material and the non-material universe, as well as the physical metaphysical nature of all humanity," showing "how to navigate that vast terrain to remove every form of chaos, pain, and suffering," according to the Los Angeles Kaballah Centre where Madonna studies.[25] A form of Jewish mysticism, Kabbalah was passed down for generations as an oral tradition. In medieval times, it became connected to the text of *The Zohar*, a collection of spiritual writings that show the way to the Light and to personal fulfillment. The Kaballah tradition is not regarded as strictly Jewish; the Kaballah Centre in Los Angeles, where Madonna and friends like Sandra Bernhard first encountered it, is open to anyone seeking spiritual guidance and self-help, including women and Christians. Some within the Jewish faith have questioned the popularization of Kaballah and its attraction for celebrities, calling it Kaballah Lite or McKaballah.[26] Madonna says that the thing that "freaks people out the most" is "having a spiritual life. That freaks people out way more than taking my clothes off and having pictures of myself taken and put into a book."[27] Her Kabbalah teacher, Rabbi Eitan Yardeni, is featured in her documentary, explaining some of its teachings. It's important, he says, to realize that every action has a consequence, "and when you understand this, you choose those thoughts that will plant positive seeds to create blessings versus chaos and negativity."

Madonna has appeared to take her study of Kaballah quite seriously, adopting the biblical name of Esther as her Kabbalah name and even visiting the tomb of a revered rabbi, Rav Ashtug, in the Occupied Zone when she was in Israel at the end of her *Re-Invention* tour during the High Holy Days in 2004. The red string she now wears on her left wrist is a Kaballah artifact to ward off the evil eye. Not just any piece of red string, it has been hallowed by its association with the tomb of Rachel, the matriarch of the Old Testament. The influence of Kabbalah is evident now in Madonna's concerts and performances, particularly in the background films she uses that emphasize the importance of light, which represents compassion and spiritual awakening. Madonna says in *I've Got A Secret to Tell You* that she believes "the only thing that's going to change the world is spirituality, not politics." Madonna has reportedly donated $21 million to the establishment of a Kabbalah school for children in Los Angeles called Spirituality for Kids.[28]

THE POLITICAL MADONNA

Madonna's ninth studio album, *American Life*, released in 2003, was a departure both musically and lyrically from her usual style. Collaborating again with French techno musician Mirwais Ahmadzi who had co-written *Music*, the album featured strings, acoustic guitars, and a gospel choir to carry message-laden lyrics about the American dream and its disappointments. As *Rolling* Stone commented, this is Madonna's "folk album," showing her "restyled as a pop-culture Che Guevara and antimaterialist girl, brooding about her life and the culture she's a part of."[29] Some fans objected, saying they were not expecting a political rally. Madonna does increasingly show her politics, though. She had appeared on MTV's *Rock the Vote* in 1990, wrapped in an American flag. She came out for General Wesley Clark in the Democratic presidential primaries and opposed reelection for President George W. Bush, urging her fans to see Michael Moore's *Fahrenheit 9/11*. The antiwar message and graphic violence of the video, *American Life*, made it controversial in the United States, and Madonna tamed it down for European release, saying that she did not intend to be critical of her country or the president (the Dixie Chicks were not so circumspect). The album met with many negative reviews and was the lowest-selling of her career, although it did get to Number One on the *Billboard* album chart initially.

At the MTV Music Awards that year, Madonna performed with Britney Spears, Christina Aguilera, and Missy Elliot, singing a remix of her song, "Hollywood." The full-on mouth kiss Madonna bestowed on Britney in front of everyone generated plenty of press and speculation. Madonna said simply that she felt very protective of Britney and saw her as a little sister. When Lourdes told her mother that "they say you are gay because you kissed Britney Spears," Madonna said, "No, it just means I kissed Britney Spears. I am the mommy pop star and she is the baby pop star. And I am kissing her to pass my energy on to her."[30] Madonna does seem very much interested in helping younger pop singers and had signed Canadian singer Alanis Morrisette to her Maverick label before she sold it, as well as the band, Prodigy.

CHILDREN'S BOOKS BY MADONNA

Madonna was also launching another branch of her career, writing children's books. She signed a contract with Callaway Editions (which had produced the *Sex* book) for five books and published her first, *The English Roses*, in 2003. Illustrated by the artist Jeffrey Fulvimari, the story, according to Madonna, is about four little English schoolgirls and their envy and jealousy of another. A fairy godmother shows them how to be compassionate. The book went to the top of the *New York Times* Children's Books list when it came out. It was followed by *Mr. Peabody's Apples*, *Yakov and the Seven Thieves*, *The Adventures of Abdi*, and *Lotsa de Casha*, a story about a selfish rich man who discovers the secret to true happiness. Madonna said that her study of Kaballah inspired her to begin writing these stories, and that she first tried them out on her daughter, Lourdes, whose reaction sometimes sent her back to revise the stories. Bergdorf Goodman offered the books in a limited edition boxed set at Christmas recently for $300; the set included a signed letter from Madonna and a CD ROM of her reading each book. *The English Roses: Too Good to Be True*, a sequel to her first book, was published in time for Christmas 2006 and follows the adventures of the same four little girls.

In addition, Madonna has launched a line of English Roses clothing for little girls. Based on the book of the same name, the clothing was inspired by Lourdes, Madonna says, and includes footwear, dolls, tea sets, charm bracelets and a musical jewelry box. "I think it's stuff that kids will really love," she says, adding that "I wish I could fit into an English Roses outfit. I tried to squeeze into one of my daughter's shirts, and looked ridiculous. No fair!"[31] The English Roses fashions, manufactured by Lipstik, include zebra-trimmed and rose-embroidered jeans, a lavender tweed suit with trendy raw edges, and a "Slumber Party" tank top and pedal pushers. They are sold at Neiman Marcus and at Los Angeles and New York City boutiques, with a price range of $50 to $175.

I'VE GOT A SECRET TO TELL YOU

In 2004, Madonna went on tour once again with *Re-Invention* for 56 concerts in the United States and Europe. Some commented that it was Madonna's "Yes, I'm still here!" message to the world, and indeed, it racked up the highest sales of any tour that year, reprising earlier hits like "Vogue," "Holiday," "Like a Prayer," and "Into the Groove," along with "What It Feels Like for a Girl," "Die Another Day," and Madonna's version of John Lennon's "Imagine." The *Re-Invention* tour was also the basis for Madonna's second documentary, *I've Got a Secret to Tell You*, released on DVD in 2006. It shows her auditioning dancers for the tour, performing on stage in tour couture by Christian LaCroix (a lavishly beaded silver bustier), complaining about her "big fat Italian thighs," cavorting with her children and husband, visiting Jerusalem, and talking about her philosophy of life. The "secret" in the title seems essentially to be her new-found serenity, achieved through the study of Kabbalah and through her family. Her 72-year-old father is shown cultivating his grapes at the Ciccone Vineyard and Winery in upstate Michigan he has retired to (he has launched a series of wines inspired by his daughter's *Confessions* tour). He attended Madonna's concert performance in Chicago with her stepmother, and comments in the film that the show was the "most positive" one she's done. Guy Ritchie appears backstage patting Madonna's backside and calling her "Mrs. R," as well as engaging in one of his favorite sports, ju-jitsu, with some of her security men. He comes off in the film as a very grounded person amid the frenzy of a Madonna tour. In fact, he seems totally unimpressed with the whole thing. At one point, he is shown playing guitar with his friends in a pub, making a tired and bored Madonna wait to go home while he finishes playing.

MADONNA ON MARRIAGE

There have been rumors about their marriage problems, which Guy and Madonna have denied, although his father has commented that they have had some rough going. It is not easy trying to have a home life with a touring pop star, a filmmaker husband, two children, and homes on opposite sides of the Atlantic. Madonna is used to juggling life this way and Guy seems the sort of person who could handle it. Still, there are inevitable strains. "It's not easy to be married, to have a successful career, to have children, to be with someone who is as strong-willed and ambitious as I am," Madonna told *Harper's Bazaar* in March 2006. "Guy's not a househusband, and I'm not a typical wife. So you can imagine, we have our clashes. But I think we always keep our eye on the ball; that is, our marriage—the union of us, the things that we create together—is bigger than the petty fights we have." She comments that their ideas about vacations are totally different: "He loves the sea and fishing and being on a boat, outdoors, nature stuff. I'd rather go to India and check out all the temples or go to Bhutan . . . He's got to start doing more of the holidays I like."[32]

In the *I've Got a Secret to Tell You* documentary, Madonna offered her observations on relationships.

> There's no such thing as the perfect soul mate. . . . Your soul mate is the person that pushes all your buttons, pisses you off on a regular basis, and makes you face your shit. It's not easy having a good marriage But I don't want easy. Easy doesn't make you grow. Easy doesn't make you think. I thank God every day that I'm married to a man who makes me think. That's my definition of true love.

And so far, Guy Ritchie is definitely the guy for Madonna. He is not her equal, but who would be? She'd already tried marriage to a Hollywood star and had affairs with other famous men. Guy seems to have made peace with Madonna's celebrity and, in the *I've Got a Secret to Tell You* documentary, displays a benign sense of humor about it.

The three most important things in a relationship, Madonna told *Rolling Stone,* are "the ability to listen, resilience, and a sense of humor."[33] She says she thinks their relationship "came off as peculiar" in the new documentary:

> Not a typical relationship. A lot of macho men see the movie and like Guy's character because he doesn't give me any special treatment. I think we come off as a couple that has a genuine and deep connection. He is always there for me, but he's not impressed. . . . It's hard for him. He was pretty much there for a lot of my tour, but it's hard for a guy to be traipsing around the world with a girl. Nobody wants to be anybody's trailer bitch. . . . You have to be a pretty evolved man to go on the road with me and not for a moment have this glimpse of yourself as someone who's lost their identity.[34]

Confessions on a Dance Floor, Madonna's tenth studio album released in the fall of 2005, returned her to her dance and disco roots, with a decided 1970s flavor, balancing "the '80s synth pop of Madonna's early years with the futuristic, electronica-infused sound she has embraced since 1998's *Ray of Light*" and "a new-wavish energy" as *People* magazine commented.[35] The single, "Hung Up," quickly reached Number One on the *Billboard* Hot 100, tying Madonna with Elvis Presley for the most top 10 songs on the U.S. singles chart. Indeed, it has been the most successful single of her career so far. Two other singles from the album, "Sorry" and "Get Together," also made the charts, and the song, "Jump," was featured in the 2006 movie, *The Devil Wears Prada,* a good theme song for a film about a high-powered fashion editor and her fashionista minions.

NOTES

1. Andrew Morton. Madonna. (New York: St. Martin's Press, 2001). 306.

2. Barbara Victor. Goddess: Inside Madonna. (New York: Cliff Street Books/ HarperCollins, 2001). 366.

3. Ibid., 366–367.

4. Ibid., 367.

5. J. Randy Taraborrelli. Madonna: An Intimate Biography. (New York: Berkley Books/Simon & Schuster, 2002). 309–310.

6. Hamish Bowles. "Like a Duchess." Vogue, August 2005. 238.

7. Details of the wedding preparations are from Victor. 371–377.

8. Ibid., 373.

9. Ibid., 374.

10. Ibid., 371.

11. Ibid., 375.

12. Ibid., 376

13. Ibid., 377.

14. Ibid. 360.

15. Bowles, 238.

16. Ibid.

17. Ibid., 232.

18. Ibid., 239.

19. Ibid., 240, 274.

20. Quoted by Lynn Hirschberg. "The Misfit." Vanity Fair, April 1991. 198.

21. Danico Lo. "Madonna and Child: Mini-Material Girl, 9, is Lourdes of her world." New York Post, March 15, 2006. 51.

22. Quoted in Campbell Robertson. "Madonna and Friends: A Guide for Perplexed Parents." The New York Times, October 23, 2005. WK4.

23. Quoted by Neil Strauss. "How Madonna Got Her Groove Back." Rolling Stone, December 1, 2005. 133.

24. Ibid., 72.

25. The Kabbalah Centre, www.kabbalah.com. (accessed August 4, 2006).

26. Morton, 288.

27. Sarah Bailey. "Madonna's Secrets." Harper's Bazaar, March 2006. 374.

28. "Madonna (entertainer)." Wikipedia. http://en.wikipedia.org/wiki/Madonna. (accessed August 3, 2006).

29. Quoted by Strauss, 72.

30. Quoted by the Associated Press, "Madonna says daughter asked if she was gay," March 6, 2006. www.mercurynews.com (accessed August 10, 2006).

31. www.englishrosescollection.com (accessed September 23, 2006).

32. Bailey, 375.

33. Quoted by Strauss, 76.

34. Ibid.

35. Chuck Arnold. "Madonna: Confessions on a Dance Floor." People, November 2006. 49.

Chapter 10

MADONNA: WHO'S THAT GIRL?

A Madonna concert is a spectacle with a capital S: things happen all at once in every dimension on a stage built at several levels and exploding with color-changing, flashing strobe lights; a humongous screen stretching the length of the stage displays film of galloping horses, desolate third-world children, war scenes, even the x-rays of the broken bones Madonna suffered when she fell off her horse 10 months ago. Acrobats and rollerbladers cavort, dancers turn impossible moves, and Madonna herself descends, almost into the laps of the audience, in a huge glittering disco ball that opens like one of those chocolate orange candies, revealing her in quasi-dominatrix equestrian mode, cracking a horsewhip and singing "Future Lovers" from her latest album, *Confessions on a Dance Floor*.

At 47, she looks fabulous: tiny but perfect, all in black, from regulation riding hat to sleek boots.[1] The audience, a sellout crowd in Madison Square Garden, is on its feet and never sits down, roaring, arms waving at the sight of her. Madonna mounts a saddle attached like a merry-go-round steed on a steel pole, and rides it like a pro, singing "Like a Virgin," then saddles up a dancer with a bit in his mouth for another ride. On the screen behind her, huge riderless horses stamp their feet, jump, even stumble. Madonna's 2006 concert tour, *Confessions on a Dance Floor*, booked for 60 venues in the United States, Europe, Japan, and, for the first time, Russia, has already been on the road for a month, but she sure doesn't look it. This, her sixth worldwide tour, is more elaborately theatrical and entertaining than ever, taking the spectator on an emotional journey. In the documentary of her *Re-Invention* tour, on her way to the first performance in Los Angeles, Madonna admits she's very nervous. But, she says, if she thinks of her concerts as "art installations," that takes the pressure off "to achieve perfection." With her dancers in a prayer circle before the concert, Madonna prays that they will "take the people in the audience to another place and inspire them to be better people."

Good luck getting a ticket anywhere on the tour. You couldn't have scrounged one for tonight in New York City, or maybe you could for $500 or more. The Garden holds up to 40,000 people, all of them seemingly hot for Madonna. There are very few teenage wannabes in evidence, but plenty of 30- and 40-year-olds dressed in vintage Madonna outfits, wannabes all grown up, their fan-dom intact, their fingerless lace gloves, fishnets, and crucifixes proof of their loyalty. Madonna gives them only "Like a Virgin" and "Lucky Star" from her repertoire. All of the other songs are from her *Confessions on a Dance Floor* album, supplying a steady stream of 1970s-disco era dance tunes, including a *Saturday Night Fever* episode, complete with Madonna in a John Travolta white suit. Madonna has returned to her disco roots. But this time around, she did a little market research first, testing out new songs beforehand to see which to include on the album by playing them, without the vocals, in British clubs and then filming the crowd reaction. As Stuart Price, her music collaborator on the album, says, "You can work on a song for 12 hours, but I guarantee you'll know within just 10 seconds of putting it on at a club whether it works or not."[2] The songs on the *Confessions* album definitely "work."

Mirrored disco ball glitter shows up everywhere on the concert stage, even on the large cross that Madonna, wearing a crown of thorns, is strapped to for a piss-everybody-off moment (it is all about AIDS relief). Behind her, images of Saddam Hussein, George Bush, Hitler, and Stalin alternate with sad pictures of children and war scenes. Church and government officials in Rome, Germany, and Russia threatened to shut down her concert over this scene; but ultimately they did not, and once again, Madonna got lots of publicity out of the uproar. She even invited Pope Benedict to her concert in Rome (he did not accept). In Germany, the question was whether Madonna's crucifix scene was "hurtful to religious people," but prosecutors in Dusseldorf decided it was "not a criminal offense and was covered by laws protecting artistic freedom."[3] In Prague, where Madonna wanted to hold an after-party on an historic bridge, officials stepped in to stop her. A Russian gangster in Moscow threatened to kidnap Madonna's children if she went ahead with her performance; Madonna ordered up extra security. Moscow protesters stabbed and ripped up posters of Madonna, and the concert venue had to be moved to a sports stadium to allow better policing. At least in London, friendly fans at her Wembley Arena concert sang happy birthday to Madonna at her performance on August 16, her 48th birthday. "I cannot think of a better way to spend my birthday than with you tonight," Madonna responded. She said her wish for her birthday would be "world peace."[4]

The day after her Moscow concert, a lawmaker in the Russian parliament introduced a proposal to organize a space trip for Madonna in 2008, saying she had expressed a desire to be a "space tourist." The proposal was rejected, however, and the Russian space agency said there would be no seats on the Russian Soyuz spacecraft anyway until 2009.[5] Back home in Los Angeles after her last tour performance in Japan (where no one protested the crucifix scene and where Madonna sported a new blonde wig with bangs), Madonna issued a statement:

> There seem to be many misinterpretations about my appearance on the cross and I wanted to explain it myself once and for all. . . . It is no different than a person wearing a cross or "taking up the cross" as it says in the Bible. My performance is neither anti-Christian, sacrilegious or blasphemous. Rather, it is my plea to the audience to encourage mankind to help one another and to see the world as a unified whole. I believe in my heart that if Jesus were alive today he would be doing the same thing.[6]

She said the intent of the scene was to "bring attention to the millions of children in Africa who are dying every day or living without care, without medicine, and without hope," and Madonna asked people to get involved "in whatever way they can." "Please," she said, "do not pass judgment without seeing my show."

The public and religious outcry against the crucifixion scene troubled NBC television executives, who debated whether to take the scene out of their planned two-hour NBC television special about Madonna's "*Confessions* Tour Live from London," set to air in November on the night before Thanksgiving. Because of pressure from the American Family Association and Chairman Donald E. Wildmon, who said showing the scene would be "blasphemous" and that opposition toward NBC would only grow, the network finally decided to remove the scene from the broadcast.[7]

Also stirring up controversy about the *Confessions* album was the song, "Isaac," sung by an Israeli singer, Sinwani. Purportedly Madonna's Kabbalah tribute to a sixteenth-century rabbi, Yitzhak Lunja, rabbis in Israel objected to the song because Hebrew law forbids using a holy rabbi's name for profit.

The New York Post called the show "Madonna Mild," not wild.[8] It *was* a mellow performance compared to her usual shock tactics. The slowest part of the show was Madonna on guitar ("retarded," said one fan), but maybe she had to catch her breath (at one point she told the audience she'd had only three hours sleep the night before). She's been admired as having "the best body on a woman over 40," and she is indeed in amazing shape, the result of a disciplined, continuous workout schedule she never lets up on. "Physicality, feeling strong, feeling empowered was my ticket out of middle-class Midwest culture," she told *Harper's Bazaar* in 2006.

> So I equate movement and strength with freedom. I used to be a freak about doing yoga, but I had to do a lot of Pilates to rehab my shoulder joint and get the use of my arm back [after her fall from a horse]. So I really started getting into Pilates and dancing more. . . .my workouts became much more ballet-oriented, rather than the visceral, gymnastic, ashtanga yoga thing. I think it made me less muscular, believe it or not. I think a lot of it has to do with the fact that I stopped doing [yoga] and you shock your body.[9]

Her hair, now a strawberry blonde, is worn in a long Farrah Fawcett style, called the "*uber*-bitch" look by Simon Doonan, creative director for the upscale Barney's department store in Manhattan, who has featured Madonna mannequins in the store windows several times.

> This new and delicious Madge incarnation—trashy 70s hairdo, fishnets, hooker blousons, spangled shoes—feels a lot more authentic than the English lady of the manor, the Kabbalist or—most preposterous of all—the demure children's author in the print shift dress and pastel cardigan.[10]

Doonan's take on Madonna's latest chameleon image just about sums it up: she's still playing with identity, still keeping us guessing about who she really is. Her stalwart academic fan, Camille Paglia, has even warned that Madonna is in danger of turning into a Joan Crawford, "with her fascist willpower signaled by brute, staring eyes and fixed jawline."[11]

True, Madonna is as demanding and bossy as ever. She admits, "I'm a control freak."[12] "I'm tough, ambitious, and I know exactly what I want. If that makes me a bitch, okay."[13] Her list of dressing room demands for the *Confessions* tour included three Kabbalah candles (to protect and keep her safe), white roses in the dressing room (which must be all white as well, including the walls), a love seat, bottles of Kabbalah water, an Ein Gedi Dead Sea foot spa, unsalted Edamame (a type of Japanese pea), and a new toilet seat on her "loo."[14] In the documentary of the *Re-Invention* tour, her minions are shown running to and fro to supply milkshakes, popcorn (she still travels with a carry-on bag full of it), and numerous other items. Madonna writes poems to her assistants in gratitude for all this help (and pays them well, assuredly). She also writes poems to crystallize her feelings, like the one she reads in *I've Got a Secret to Tell You* that she says she wrote after being "in a very bad mood."

Like the lyrics she writes for her songs, Madonna's poems are confessional. Her song lyrics tend to document her own emotional life, an aspect of her music that is part of its appeal to her fans.

> I think most female artists are that way. Maybe not in pop music, but if you look at the work of Sylvia Plath or Frida Kahlo or the poetry of Anne Sexton, a lot of female artists take what they've experienced in their life and put it into their work. I don't think I'm so original or unusual in that respect. Maybe people aren't so used to it in pop culture.[15]

Who's that girl? She's morphing, molting, maybe turning into herself after all. Madonna will be facing 50 soon. Will she carry on like Cher or Mick Jagger, into her 60s? Or will she gracefully retire to her English estate, enjoying the wealth and leisure she's well earned over more than two decades? The biggest danger for Madonna has always been boredom; it's not clear that she could stand being out of the action for long. *New York Post* columnist Liz Smith predicts it'll be *Madonna at 80: Ready, Willing, and Still Able*.[16]

As postmodern icon, as the most successful female pop star of the twentieth century and beyond, as wife and mother, Madonna has earned her place in America's heart and around the world. Her influence on pop music is undeniable and far-reaching. New pop icons from Nelly Furtado and Shakira to Gwen Stefani and Christina Aguilera (not to mention Britney Spears) owe Madonna a debt of thanks for the template she forged, combining provocative sexiness and female power in her image, music, and lyrics.

With more than 250 million copies of her albums sold, Madonna is now "officially the most successful international female solo artist in the world, ever," the Web site AbsoluteMadonna.com breathlessly announced during her 2006 *Confessions* tour.[17] The tour itself is the highest-grossing tour ever by a female artist, earning $193.7 million from 60 shows that drew 1.2 million fans.[18] The *Guinness Book of World Records* in 2000 declared her the most successful female recording artist of all time. In the United States, Madonna has had 27 Top 20s singles, setting a record for a female artist. Twelve of these, including 10 she wrote or co-wrote herself, went to Number One on the charts. The *Hung Up* video from her *Confessions* album has received five MTV Award nominations: Video of the Year, Best Female Video, Best Dance Video, Best Pop Video, and Best Choreography. Her song, "Hung Up," made the *Billboard* Hot 100, tying her with Elvis Presley for the most Top 10 songs on the U.S. singles chart (Madonna has always found it significant that the anniversary of Elvis's death is her birthday, August 16). She is the richest female singer in the world, with an estimated net worth of $850 million.[19]

Where does she go from here? Madonna is apparently not quite done with the movies, and will play Princess Selenia in *Arthur and the Invisibles*, a live action and animated film based on the children's book by Luc Bresson, to be released by the Weinstein Company in 2007. But, as she told Liz Smith, what's she'd really like to do is direct.[20] Madonna also partnered with the trendy Swedish H&M stores (Hennes & Mauritz) to wear H&M clothes off stage during her tour and to design a special Madonna tracksuit (very slimming, in black, white, or purple) that is sold at H&M stores. She, her music collaborator, and her dancers also modeled in H&M ads (she had already appeared in a series of ads for the Gap in 2003).[21] She is starting her own line of clothing, M by Madonna, to be sold through H&M stores.

Madonna has announced that her next big charity project will be helping orphans in Africa, where AIDS has left more than a million children without a parent in the southeastern country of Malawi. She plans to raise $3 million to begin providing care for these children and has enlisted the help of the William J. Clinton Foundation. In a letter on her Web site, www.madonna.com, Madonna writes that the project "is very close to my heart, a new effort to bring an end to the extreme poverty and degradation endured by Malawi's orphans."[22]

Madonna and her husband Guy went to Malawi in the fall of 2006 to visit an orphanage with plans to adopt a child (like Brad Pitt and Angelina Jolie). They set their sights on a 13-month-old motherless boy, David Banda, and whisked him off to their home in London before the Malawi authorities could begin their usual 18-to-24-month assessment of the parents. Though the Ritchies had an interim adoption order from a Malawi judge, this move caused considerable commotion, and Madonna appeared on *The Oprah Winfrey Show* and in interviews on the *Today* show and *Dateline NBC* to explain it all ("I hope to be the mother that I didn't have," she told Meredith Viera). She issued an "Open Letter" to her fans on her website, which stated in part:

> My husband and I began the adoption process many months prior to our trip to Malawi. I did not wish to disclose my

intentions to the world prior to the adoption happening as this is a private family matter . . . . . we have gone about the adoption procedure according to the law like anyone else who adopts a child. Reports to the contrary are totally inaccurate.[23]

As it turned out, the Malawi Ministry of Women and Child Welfare, which has been monitoring the adoption and David's life in London, reported in January 2007 that "so far we see a loving mother in Madonna, and David is very fine."[24] Malawi officials said they will continue to monitor the family and David as part of the adoption process. Malawi rights groups who protested the swift adoption appear to have been mollified.

WHO'S THAT GIRL?

There can be only one Madonna. Her public identity as an artist is well established; in performance, her many-sided and changing image fascinates and energizes our cultural moment. Madonna is not the product of some music industry idea, but her own woman. She is still driven to achieve: "Even though I've become Somebody, I still have to prove that I'm *Somebody*. My struggle has never ended and it probably never will."[25] From the first, Madonna herself has created her own image, expressing in her music a compelling emotional life. That seems to resonate with the audience. She's been the soundtrack for their lives and the queen of an entertainment culture where visual image reigns. "My sister is her own masterpiece," her brother Christopher says. "Is there any other way to do it right?"[26]

Certainly part of her legacy will be her validation of young women's aspirations, showing them that they can have freedom and control over their lives as women. In all of her transformations, a fan points out that

> [N]early every fan has seen a glimmer of herself, or himself, reflected in her at some point . . . Whether she was celebrating interracial relationships, gay club culture or S-and-M, the spirit of her work has always been inclusive. To see even a part of yourself embraced by her, especially a part that you feel is marginalized, can be a heady validation.[27]

Still it's the private person we wish we could discover. What's she really like? Celebrities fight a constant battle to keep their private lives separate from their public life, and Madonna is no different.

The only thing she has is who she really is.

Perhaps what Madonna has been trying to tell us all along is that identity *is* a performance, a portrayal of self that each of us enacts every day.

Strike a pose!

NOTES

1. W magazine featured 58 pages of photographs of Madonna in equestrienne mode in its September 2006 issue.

2. Stephanie Goodman. "Dance-Floor Focus Group." The New York Times, August 3, 2005. D2.

3. "Madonna, Pro and Con." The New York Times, August 22, 2006. D2.

4. "Madonna's Birthday Treat From Audience." www.madonna.com (accessed August 18, 2006).

5. Associated Press. "Proposal for Madonna Space Trip Rejected." September 13, 2006. www.absolutemadonna.com. (accessed September 22, 2006).

6. Spiegelman, Arthur. "Madonna Defends Being 'Crucified' on Stage." Reuters News Agency. September 21, 2006. http://news.aol.com. (accessed September 22, 2006).

7. "NBC Backs Off Madonna Crucifix Scene." www.absolutemadonna.com (accessed September 22, 2006).

8. Dan Aquilante. "Madonna & mild at MSG." The New York Post, June 29, 2006. 79.

9. Quoted by Sarah Bailey. "Madonna's Secrets." Harper's Bazaar, March 2006. 373.

10. Simon Doonan. "Ta-Ta, Dull Do-Gooders: All Hail the New Virago." *The New York Observer*, December 12, 2005. 10.

11. Camille Paglia. www.salon.com December 2005. Quoted by Doonan, 10.

12. Neil Strauss. "How Madonna Got Her Groove Back." *Rolling Stone*, December 1, 2005. 74.

13. Quoted in The Guerrilla Girls. *Bitches, Bimbos and Ballbreakers: The Guerrilla Girls' Illustrated Guide to Female Stereotypes*. (New York: Penguin Books, 2003). 25.

14. "Madonna's Dressing Room Demands." www.absolutemadonna.com (accessed August 8, 2006).

15. Quoted by Bailey, 374.

16. Liz Smith. "No Quitting for me or Madge." *The New York Post*, June 29, 2006. 24.

17. "News." www.absolutemadonna.com (accessed August 18, 2006).

18. Spiegelman. "Madonna Defends Being 'Crucified' on Stage."

19. "Madonna's Achievements." www.absolutemadonna.com (accessed September 22, 2006).

20. Smith, 24.

21. Robert Murphy. "Madonna to Don H&M Duds on Tour." *Women's Wear Daily*, June 9, 2006). 3.

22. "Madonna Finds a Cause." www.madonna.com (accessed August 4, 2006).

23. "An Open Letter from Madonna." October 17, 2006. www.madonna.com (accessed October 20, 2006).

24. "Malawi Issues Madonna's Report Card." *The New York Times*. January 8, 2006. B2.

25. Quoted by Lynn Hirshberg. "The Misfit." *Vanity Fair*, April 1991. 198.

26. *Ibid.*, 160.

27. Stephanie Rosenbloom. "Defining Me, Myself, and Madonna." *The New York Times Sunday Styles*, November 13, 2005. 2.

SELECTED BIBLIOGRAPHY

Articles, Books, and Documentaries by Madonna

The Adventures of Abidi. New York: Callaway Editions, 2004.
The English Roses: Too Good to Be True. New York: Callaway Editions, 2006.
The English Roses. New York: Callaway Editions, 2003.
I've Got a Secret to Tell You. Directed by Jonas Akerland. Lucky Lou Productions/Warner Bros., 2005.
Lotsa de Casha. New York: Callaway Editions, 2005.
"The Madonna Diaries." *Vanity Fair*, November 1996: 174–188, 223–232.
Mr. Peabody's Apples. New York: Callaway Editions, 2003.
Sex. New York: Warner Books, 1992.
Truth or Dare. Directed by Alek Keyshishian. Miramax, 1990.
Yakov and the Seven Thieves. New York: Callahan Editions, 2004.

Books about Madonna

Andersen, Christopher. *Madonna Unauthorized*. New York: Island Books/Dell Publishing, 1991.
Faith, Karlene. *Madonna: Bawdy & Soul*. Toronto:University of Toronto Press, 1997.
Guilbert, Georges-Claude. *Madonna as Postmodern Myth*. Jefferson, N.C.: McFarland & Company, 2002.
Matthew-Walker, Robert. *Madonna*. London: Pan Books/Sidgwick & Jackson, Limited., 1991.
Metz, Allan and Carol Benson, Eds. *Madonna Companion*. New York: Schirmer Books, 1999.
Morton, Andrew. *Madonna*. New York: St. Martins, 2001.
Schwichtenberg, Cathy, Ed. *The Madonna Connection: Representational Politics, Subcultural Identities, and Cultural Theory*. Boulder, Col.: Westview Press, 1993.

St.Michael, Mick. *Madonna Talking: Madonna in Her Own Words*. London: Omnibus Press, 1999.

Taraborrelli, J. Randy. *Madonna: An Intimate Biography*. New York: Berkley Books/Simon & Schuster, 2002.

Victor, Barbara. *Goddess: Inside Madonna*. New York: Cliff Street Books/HarperCollins, 2001.

Voller, Debbi. *Madonna: The Style Book*. London: Omnibus Press, 1999.

Articles about Madonna

Bailey, Sarah. "Madonna's Secrets." *Harper's Bazaar*, March 2006, 360–75.

Bowles, Hamish. "Like a Duchess." *Vogue*, August 2005, 230–40; 274.

Hirschberg, Lynn. "The Misfit." *Vanity Fair*, April 1991. 158–68; 196–202.

Orth, Maureen. "Madonna in Wonderland." *Vanity Fair*, October 1992. 204–13; 298–306.

Robertson, Campbell. "Madonna and Friends: A Guide for Perplexed Parents." *New York Times*, October 23, 2005. WK4.

Smith, Liz. "Listen, Look Beyond Crucifix." *New York Post*, May 25, 2006. www.nypost.com/gossip/liz.

_____. "No Quitting for me or Madge." *New York Post*, June 29, 2006. 24.

Strauss, Neil. "How Madonna Got Her Groove Back." *Rolling Stone*, December 1, 2005. 70–76; 133.

Books on Music History, Postmodern Theory, and Feminism

Bayles, Martha. *Hole in Our Soul: The Loss of Beauty and Meaning in American Popular Music*. New York: The Free Press/Macmillan, Inc., 1994.

Butler, Judith. *Gender Trouble: Feminism and the Subversion of Identity*. New York: Routledge, 1990.

Debord, Guy. *Society of the Spectacle*. Detroit: Black and Red, 1983.

Harvey, David. *The Condition of Postmodernity*. Oxford: Basil Blackwell, Ltd., 1990.

Jameson, Frederic. *Postmodernism, or, The Cultural Logic of Late Capitalism*. Durham, N.C.: Duke University Press, 1991.

Paglia, Camille. *Sex, Art, and American Culture*. New York: Vintage Books, 1993.

Internet

Ciccone, Silvio. *Ciccone Vineyards*. www.cicconevineyards.com

Cocks, Jay. "These Big Girls Don't Cry." *Time*, March 4, 1985. www.time.com

Gravelle, Maruice. "Madonna Career Diary." www.absolutemadonna.com

"Madonna." *Wikipedia*. www.wikipedia.org

Madonna's Web site: www.madonna.com

Sischy, Ingrid. "Letter from the Editor." *Interview*, March 2001. www.interview.com

Skow, John. "Madonna Rocks the Land." *Time*, May 27, 1985. www.time.com

Worrell, Denise. "Now: Madonna on Madonna." *Time*, May 27, 1985. www.time.com

INDEX